Leonard Cohen

YESTERDAY'S TOMORROW

A highly original look back and forward

Marc Hendrickx

Bookline and Thinker

*Dedicated to Varlam Sjalomov (1907–1982)*

*symbol of human impotence and hope*

First published by Uitgeverij Van Halewyck, 2004
Translated from Dutch by Annmarie Sauer, 2005
Published Brandl & Schlesinger, Australia, 2008

Published by Bookline & Thinker Ltd, 2019
7 Regent Court
OX7 5PJ
www.booklinethinker.com

A CIP catalogue for this book is available from the British Library.

ISBN: 9781916410350

Cover design by More Visual Ltd.

CONTENTS

## Context

Whether you have followed the life and work of Leonard Cohen for decades or discovered him during his recent resurgence, you may find yourself looking back to his earlier life and work.

Incredible as it may seem, but Cohen's career – for want of another word, as the man himself despised the term – has taken steep surges and declines. For instance, before his resurgence in 2008, he had become a virtual non-performer. His reputation and fame had been greatly diminished. However, this wasn't the first time this happened. Critics had written Cohen off twice before. First as early as 1970, when he struggled with what he intensely strived to be – a poet and a writer. The stark contrast of this quest helped make him popular. However, it brought Cohen anxiety, fears and depression to a point where he could no longer write, let alone sing or perform as the pop world expected him to do. A little over a decade later Cohen poured his heart and soul into a collection of psalms, *Book of Mercy*, and an album, *Various Positions*. Both received a lukewarm response, at best. In the U.S., Cohen's record company CBS did not even deem *Various Positions* worthy of release. However, the album contains such classic material that its reception stands as a telling testimony to the qualities of the music press and those in charge of the music industry

For me, thirty years Mr. Cohen's junior, his work has been a constant source of inspiration. Likewise, the way in which it was perceived, proved beyond anything that the degree of success a book, play or recording enjoys is anything but related to its qualities. Success is ephemeral. The result of a number of issues which surround any given release. Godawful material can sell in vast quantities. Beautiful work might remain dormant on a shelve.

When I started to write the first edition of *Yesterday's Tomorrow*, the context was crucially important. Leonard Cohen was regarded as a has-been. His work cast aside. Over and done with. Which, to me, offered perfect circumstances to delve deep. I wanted to look into Cohen's body of work in order to find its true value, and whether these items from Yesterday held a Tomorrow. A worth that could possibly make them last, regardless of their has-been status. Having come in direct contact with the artist through mail, I was pleased to have him give me permission *'from one writer to another'* to study his work, evaluate it, confront it, and – in the end – publish the outcome of my findings.

In doing so I worked hard to deliver a book that would do justice to the creative efforts Leonard Cohen put into his work for over half a century. I have tried to use my experiences as a writer from a different generation and background to act as a mirror. It goes without saying that in the end, *Yesterday's Tomorrow* proves just how valuable the texts were.

However, that proved to be just the beginning.

First, my book and its insights became far more popular than I had ever dared to imagine. Editions in Flemish, Dutch, Spanish, Portuguese and English were welcomed by eager audiences all over the globe. Then, the man himself added a new and most surprising dimension to his old work. From 2008 onwards he returned with a new lease of life, announcing a massive string of concerts, which were met with unprecedented success. Alongside this, Cohen added new material to his already existing and impressive catalogue, further expanding on his favorite themes. Let's again take a look at Cohen's most impressive work and share thoughts on the depth and intensity of his words.

Marc Hendrickx

## PREMISE

*'Great men are usually first understood when framed by the perspective of years. Something to give them perspective is necessary. The world is far-sighted and always confused by what takes place under its nose.'*

Robert W. Chambers

As the biographer of a few lives I am inclined to subscribe to the statement above from Robert Chambers. When writing a biography, it's easy to fall into silly romanticism over the subject's birth house and hair locks and wanting to own it all. But I always guarded against delivering a glossy biography by triple jumping through anecdotes and quotations, and including a hagiography or academic parlando.

*Yesterday's Tomorrow* is not the definitive biography. Nor is it an artist's life, reduced to words, but a confrontation, looking at Cohen's balancing act between humor and tragedy, between ambitious dreams and pathetic failures, between a big heart and willpower, at the same time weak and strong.

This is not a book of open literary pretensions. It is humble. Literature without pretense. There are no direct answers, as they are often wrong anyway. A sentimental journey? Perhaps, if you manage to erase the negative connotation sentimentality evokes. Yet in a strange way this characterization fits this small story. After all, it draws from the literal and philosophical experiences of roaming lives and the nagging feeling that the shadow side of these lives etched its pattern more sharply than the lighter side. Carefully it registers the consequences of smaller internal and external explosions, while details are enlarged so that the totality of these details seem to suggest a more friendly human existence, averse to rarefied romanticism.

Through the years Leonard Cohen often characterized his

writing as a choice of life. Here, on these pages, I openly profess the same conviction. Like Cohen, I will go on searching, toiling if need be, for subjects that are important to me and about which I need to write. Here and there in a light tone, of course, but without degenerating into the all too common banter passed off by some as reporting, I would like to keep conscience and a soul.

*If you miss the train I'm on*
*You will know that I am gone*
*You can hear the whistle blow a hundred miles*
*A hundred miles, a hundred miles,*
*a hundred miles, a hundred miles*
*You can hear the whistle blow*
*a hundred miles*

Hedy West – Jacques Plante – Traditional

Chapter 1

THE GUESTS

*'Midway this way of life we're bound upon I woke to find myself in a dark wood, where the right road was wholly lost and gone.'* It could have been a direct quote. But today, some seventy years after Leonard Norman Cohen let out his first scream in this world, the healing, prophetic poet looks back mildly. His *Divine Comedy* is nearly accomplished. Yours truly on the other hand, still only stands at the fringe of the dark forest. The realm of thinkers still out of reach.

In the past I wrote about larger than life figures, important organizations or themes. Each time I clarified the world in which they moved, their drives and impact. To me, it was about an almost instinctive form of recognition. I know my subjects. Little else do I believe so intensely and with such a demanding force. An attuned soul like Leonard Cohen shares the same territory; he uses language I understand and highlights feelings which mirror my own. That is our bond. And even though I am prone to some mild admiration, I am also able to put things into perspective, a trait that is a consequence of meeting the man himself when he turned up, out of the blue, on my doorstep. No one at that age expects to be important enough to see one of his role models show up at the front door. Another result of that encounter is that I always gave my biographical subjects enough breathing space to allow each reader with a bit of common sense to do his own filling in rather than strictly delineated reporting. Squelching a rich life with a truckload full of facts and present it as a biography or study – no thanks! Allow me to classify that kind of approach as an act of suffocating love.

I have worked for many years with the man who gave the world *Marianne* and *Suzanne*, who compared the hopeless

3

quest of people to a bird on a wire and who warns and comforts. Seldom do his lyrics and music leave my cocoon. His quotes grace my publications. But today I set Leonard Cohen free. Here on the pages of this book you will not find 'my' Leonard Cohen, rather the precipitation of what his oeuvre released in me, together with a hundred-and-one other events that mark a man's life. What you are reading now is not easily classified in a thematic box. It is a mosaic without a real beginning or end. Narrative prose, in which different sequences find their place intuitively rather than in an efficient and planned way. Call it a song, with a text structured in wide stanzas and with musical variations upon different themes.

The core of this project, the alpha and omega, lies in what I share with Leonard Cohen. Most importantly, we are both writers. Cohen is not the kind of man with an all-encompassing theorem. He holds no *'le génie, sinon rien'* (genius or nothing) attitude. Nor are generalizations his thing. Truth is far too complex for that. Leonard Cohen: *'I'm a serious writer. I believe in the value of high seriousness, especially in a public culture which is devoted to frivolity and distraction. We do live in a moral universe. There is a judgment. We all live the life of the heart, people do take their lives seriously.'*

This is what you do as an author. Daily. Time and again you choose that one unavoidable direction: the truth. Even if it is often confrontational or uncomfortable in one way or another. Principles and dedication drive you. The promise has to be kept, regardless of whether it counts. Your whole being demands the job be done well, that the task gets fulfilled. The biggest help in this is plain seriousness. Seriousness, so often damned for being the one element that keeps you from carefree diversions. The same seriousness with which Leonard Cohen follows his course. A path shared for a long time. You know it brings results, even if you do not always have the spirit of the time on your side.

That last point is not unimportant. Though it may rather limit your oeuvre in size, that one element makes a larger

4

production fairly impossible. With Cohen I learned that, besides the awareness of your talent to realize something, you need an exceptionally clear understanding of your own shortcomings, weaknesses, inconsistencies and lapses. The mood changes with emphasis and regularity. Ambition in the things you do becomes your lot. Murderous doubts too, as well as moments of poisoned reflection. Power and powerlessness become your drives, if it is not your eternal lover – of that point in time – who spurs on the horse or hobbles it.

Something else we share is our wish to revisit. Revisit authenticity. Revisit a person. Revisit an influence, a language, and roots. The eternal homecoming. While for me this is almost exclusively related to my creative work and partners, the singer poet also opts for an outspoken life with God. A choice some less well informed at times relate to his classical Jewish upbringing. Actually, it goes much further and deeper in Cohen, transcending form. His *If It Be Your Will* is telling. A prayer, in complete devotion. Hope has been transformed into belief. Dignity replaces shame. Call whom is spoken to God, Yahweh, Allah or whatever, Cohen prays to him for reconciliation and unity in true love.

Texts about love exist in many shades. But discussion of the complex, the hows and whys, the challenges and the solutions offered, however, is fairly rare. If the addressee happens to be the ultimate Supreme Being, most pen pushers are easily reduced to stereotypes. Not so Leonard Cohen. He is open, honest, and direct. His heart so big that whoever is spoken to comes across as a living God, a believable and laudable participant in the conversation. Because of this, for creative spirits like Leonard Cohen, the dilemma is whether to kick people into having a conscience or leave them to their own selves; and this becomes relegated to a distant second place way after their own struggle. A struggle with the subject matter, with our position as human beings and with ourselves.

To use Thoreau's credo: *'Great God, I ask thee for no meaner pelf than that I may not disappoint myself.'* It is a troublesome but unavoidable choice. It offers the author and human being a clear outline where many, purposefully or overcome by human deficit, opt for a limited and vague life.

Choosing the other road and defining one's own path, one uses life, experiences and subconscious as a basis. Leonard Cohen is not an intellectual who, for a fleeting moment, descends from his cloud in order to meditate about the world. He wants to listen, take classes in reality. Doing so he stumbles through life, as we all do.

Cohen continuously tries to break through the ossification, the rigidity we ourselves have brought to life. A choice by and for the individual. You do not draw a barrier around your flaws, nor do you try to sublimate them by your art. You accept the confrontation! This confrontation, the core of Cohen's existence, does not even remotely resemble the abject clichés that pretend to represent the singer-poet: The decadent poser. The charlatan with neurotic pulses. The man who wholesales in melancholy and 'tristesse'. The pessimism guru with depressing morals.

The author watches, listens and registers. He knows and makes his point without whining. That does not make his writing optimistic. Cohen is not the type to evangelize encouraging enthusiasm that gives meaning to life, like Dom Helder Camara. He is no velvet rebel à la Oscar Wilde. Even less is he prone to turning bourgeois – that on-going stultification of the senses. His role is that of the observer. An observer who wants to see life as it is, not as it should be. Cohen not only wants to experience. Above all he wants to grasp the sense of things. That is the message he brings. He calls this *'to report'*. Not without the necessary eloquence, but unadorned. Sharp, lucid. Not sarcastic, seldom cynical, he manages without effort to lay bare the emotional suffering of the middle class.

His work speaks for many, yet Cohen is no thief of any other person's feelings. His poetry and music do not constitute a culturally safe recreation of the world, rather an imagination that softens our perception musically and sharpens it through the lyrics. His voice consecrates, his lyrics are of brimstone and fire. Ambiguity is omnipresent, depth an absolute necessity. Luckily, his wisdom does not stand in the way of occasional humor. It is only seemingly difficult to reconcile the different visions on Leonard Cohen: the poet and the critical observer, the lonely heart and the one knowing women, the ascetic and the lover of exquisite wines, the downcast author, and the warm spirited personality. Consider the life and work of the artist with a bit more than casual attention and have some feeling for the rich nuances offered by a truly lived inner life, and you will immediately grasp an exceptionally acceptable total image. A man of evolutions, developments and restless growth, matched to a strong inner force.

As an author one may want to work from his or her own human point of view; yet being a writer unavoidably colors your vision and your life. Having said that, it does not dominate all and everything. There always remains a trace of the man as a human being. And then there are the other people. Even if those he consciously spends time with are often also very driven. They virtually have to be. Without purpose, work or framework you would fall back upon yourself and your direct surroundings. Too limited a world of experience for an obsessed individual. If you want to continue blackening pages, having a broad spectrum is a necessity. The past almost always being colored by the present. Almost. Once in a while a crazed freak appears.

A person who tries to approach the original circumstances as closely as possible and rips open the frazzled seams. Each time it becomes clear how much observations and perceptions are subject to change. People look at you in astonishment... 'Was it like that?' For a moment a pleasant feeling. Then you break. What is the specific gravity of what you have come to know? What happiness can be bought with the knowledge that each individual artist's life deserves more than a superficial approach?

An aesthete of memory constantly readjusts the rear-view

mirror of life. At the age of twenty-five, who among us really contemplates his past? Drawn by the siren song of the past, framed with the melancholy color of loss. You look at the sky, at a star, light-years away. How you would like to stand on one of the accompanying planets, look at the earth and know that all your heroes are still alive, young and in their prime? And looking back alone is not enough. No, it is not even really about you, yourself, but rather about that indefinable 'us.' Who are we? Where do we come from? What influences help define that process?

When confronted with the past, most people only want to see what is beautiful. Others cannot distance themselves from it quickly enough. And yet, without true memory there is no life. Still, only a minority is able to really look what happened in the face, unselfish and unattached, looking for the invisible lessons that every experience brings. To me it is a way of explaining who I am. Put the finger on the wound and push hard. Accentuate sickness, ugliness and decline. Speak about death and oblivion. About jealousy, lack of love, frustration. Distance is important. That distance, in space and in time, is necessary in order to report correctly and completely.

I realize that dealing in memories, in words, is typically Jewish. I also know the risk that becoming a memory junkie holds, becoming caught in the long tentacles of tradition, the drama of missed opportunities. When does an event become a memory? I wonder. I am very much aware that we do not know our times. At least not in the way our descendants will know them. I have seen more than enough proof of that. But as long as stories help define the landscape of our memory, I will go on telling them regardless, true and with integrity. If need be against the tide.

Today the media fulfil the role of short-term memory. They spout stories, define the course of the river. Though the phenomenon is not new, it is pretty determining. He who stands in his work with an acute sense of time sees and feels how the field of tension stretches out over several decades. How each event is tributary to it. Big time reputations are made and undone on page one with the same casualness as the umpteenth item about people celebrating their marriage jubilee that is laid to rest way back in the regional pages.

Knowing that human beings – depending upon the circumstances in which they function, the way they perceive themselves and whether or not they can live with this self-image – are capable of staggering magnificence, is a thought that keeps you going. When under that influence you believe that you can tip your personal balance in the right direction. If it does not work out that way, you are left merely with ugliness, imperfection and an immense shortcoming, tearing you apart. Whatever the result, you learn. You win at every turn.

And so, you try to build the only right bridge between your not yet stylized notes and the impossible task that has for years spoiled your life and poisoned your brain. Over and over. In this way, all your work eventually turns into one book, one entity. You put so much in it from yourself, always and forever hoping to catch and pass on a glimpse of what you have been chasing for years, that such has become unavoidable.

This book deals with man, his life and fate. It considers the position of the individual in the world, in happiness, in awakening to consciousness, descent, faith, mission, love, old age and death. Antiquated concepts? Not really. Even if we accept that we are all damaged angels, there is no escaping them. In the end we create our own truth. Not exactly because we look for it with conviction, but rather because we mirror each other and the world. Alas, many of our sources are suspect and our opinions are often influenced, directly or indirectly. The freedom people can win by amassing wisdom is hard to handle for a great many among them. They prefer to drift in idleness or escape into replacement filler activities. And there are enough Pharisees providing those these days.

Almost behind every word consigned to us, cash registers can be heard ringing. Society grants the individual person only a right to exist as a potential consumer. For the rest his or her singularity is negated, crushed under tons of commercial messages, incentives and quasi-obligations. Buying normal, everyday bread has become difficult. It has to be multi-grain bread, gluten bread or what-the-hell-s**t-bread ever, if you are lucky enough for your daily food not to have the name of a TV or cartoon personality. Those who have no talent, have not a single idea and no spark shining through at all, seem exclusively occupied with the editing of senseless magazines or the production of shameless exploitation TV nowadays.

Even in the once so rigorous world of books they have made their less than glorious appearance: the smiling dictators of commercial fun and games, the empty-headed nothing, the slick, limited life. Sartre said: *'Hell are the others.'* He could have added that you cannot get away from people who want to prove *ad infinitum just* how hellish they are. On television, on the web, in the street, on paper. Everywhere they show how bewilderingly banal and stupid they are, ready to manipulate and be manipulated. The hell they create is called voyeurism, with a shot of self-conceit on top.

Strange how your mind afflicts you. I cannot help but wonder if these people ever reach the point where they become conscious that they are one hundred percent guaranteed fake. As if a person does not have other ghosts to chase, even if they are only his own fears and delusions. How to handle freedom? How to handle our life? The individual decides. With Cohen we ask the question whether we create our own truth or let it be made for us. Or do we forsake it? Countless people do not even get to make that decision. They become fatally ensnared in their own life, blind to the fact that they are the authors of their own drama. In their head reigns oppressive inevitability and loss of control. They harbor these feelings because they allow them to say: 'It is not my fault that this is happening; can I help it?'

A relief, yet at the same time a source of self-inflicted pain. You can certainly be in control. Make choices. He or she who looks under the thin veneer knows that nobody escapes the consequences of his acts.

Could I, knowing this, conceive a plan to write this book? *'The devil laughs when you make plans'*, the proverb says. Yet there are also words by Leonard, sententious as ever: *'The heart is always involved with wishing, wanting, longing, possessing, holding, losing. That's the landscape of the heart... It is important that the real feelings in society and the life of the heart be affirmed.'* Cohen and I have an *'ensouled connection'*, to quote Marsman. Maybe this book's goal is to found a community of *solitaires*. Wouldn't that be a wonderful paradox? *Join the club, please.*

No kidding: the writer knows, feels, sharper than others, that life only brings disillusions: your parents die, you lose friends, a child becomes estranged, your health fails, love turns into a disaster. All the while, duty calls. That eternal fork in the road. Your own small trail of slime. In literature, maybe only in the margins of literature. Negligibly minimal. At the same time, we see a thousand-fold what any committee member, any hollow literary keg can crowd together. So you go for it.

Without disdain I dare claim that this is an engaged book; even if engagement seems to have become a contaminated concept. Let's say that it is not value free. A soft book? Hard ideas?

Sometimes. First and foremost, let it be a penetrating allegory. A license. To think about, to classify vertically, to work with actively, to question, to know that the author is possessed by a slogan that hardly subtly demands its freedom.

Karl Marx ended the intro of *Das Kapital* with *'I know that all kinds of people will attack this work. I did what I could and thus I think of Dante's line: Follow your path and just let people prattle away.'*

In the light of a flickering torch *The Guests* displays exceptional compassion. Empathy with those who have, empathy with those who have *not*. An invitation to each person, regardless his or her passion. Welcome, welcome!

*One by one The Guests arrive*
*The Guests are coming through*
*The open-hearted many*
*The broken-hearted few*

*One by one The Guests arrive*
*The Guests are coming through*
*The broken-hearted many*
*The open-hearted few*
Leonard Cohen

Chapter 2

## MAZ'L TOV!

We wish it to each other without thinking, in all degrees and in all possible situations. At the same time the concept is so vague we can hardly use it at all. Happiness. Under that heading, probably the most inconsistent emotions and feelings that a human can register lie hidden. Nothing is only good or bad. Nothing is approved without fuss by the arch-enemies reason and feeling. And how often does a feeling of happiness not follow a moment of contained tragedy? Schopenhauer, misanthropic philosopher if there ever was one, even believed that we humans are not capable of true happiness. This made Nietzsche qualify him as *'a coward who wants to live like a frightened doe in the woods'*.

If we enter the woods unafraid, then we can only conclude that the individual hardly questions the meaning of individual existence, as long as the community in which this person lives is close knit and functions as a solid block. It is different when traditions become lost and communities crumble into desolate anonymity. Call it 'now'. We are full of ourselves, see only the sovereign, almost godless 'I,' while Marx already understood that we confuse freedom often with free trade. We are free, as long as we stay within the well-travelled paths of our society based on production and consumption. The natural longing for a meaningful life has been perverted into a desperate obligation to be happy and to radiate happiness. Real, spiritual happiness is pursued by far fewer candidates.

Meanwhile, the time spent questioning whether what you are, and whether what you really have is what you always wanted, is lost in advance. It seems better to pursue a more realistic ambition. Rebelling against the conformity of happiness and balancing your life on your own strength for example. Trying to live twenty thousand days of your existence consciously seems a noble aim. The strength and the weakness of people who succeed in doing this is that they are single individuals. Willem Frederik Hermans wrote, *'I do not know what is worse: being alone and thinking that you are alone, or knowing that everybody is just as lonely.'*

A truth, unavoidable like the sun and as scorching, is turned to his advantage by Leonard Cohen. Cohen gives absolute priority to the individual and reduces the community to nothing more than the willing result of all these individualities. One cannot build communal structures that way? The singer-poet will probably never reach an advanced state of integration in society. For that he pleads too much radical independence and a decided unwillingness to take a position. *Various Positions* was not an accidental title. Those who profess fixed points of view get into trouble. A free human being questions what is in the air. He or she accepts *le mal de vivre,* is aware of, and thinks through the feeling of only fitting in this existence with difficulty, living in and with the knowledge that the most valuable things in life are not happiness and joy, but a deeper fulfilment that is experienced when a hurdle thought to be unassailable has been overcome or a sheer unattainable goal has been reached. His or her happiness has a contrary beauty, not always fitting the reigning customs or accepted patterns.

Leonard Cohen regularly repeats: *'This is a serious business, this existence of ours.'* His seriousness refers to the only thing of value a human has as long as he or she is allowed to dwell on this earth: life itself. As a sub-current you hear that it is pointless to explicitly strive for happiness. You think. You do not leave that to others. What is more, if you want to be more or less human you think constantly. How do you explain simplicity? What road to take to be *'free as running water'*?

Thus you start searching. You make a voyage.

Chapter 3

LE RADEAU DE LA MÉDUSE

*O jours si pleins d'appas*
*Oh days, so full of wonder*
*Vous êtes disparus*
*You have disappeared*
*Et mon pays, hélas*
*And my country, unfortunately*
*Je ne le verrai plus*
*I will see no more*
M.A. Gerin-Lajoie

The central myth in our culture is the expulsion of mankind from paradise. We do not live in the Garden of Eden. Human impotence to handle this knowledge is a source of endless suffering. Too often something or somebody stands up promising the return to paradise: an institution or a person, a party, a church or a charismatic holy leader. Dangerous people for the most part, who want to create their own small paradise and happen to have a suitable dialectic at their disposal. Cohen's vision? In one of his songs we hear, *'Follow me, the wise man said, but he walked behind.'*

Man as a plaything of fate? Destined to wander? Our quest seems endless and maybe we will never truly know who we are, floating around on that sheer endless ocean, the cosmos of our life. It is not necessarily a hopeless image. It is a vision. Man travelling, becoming what he must. In Leonard Cohen's case a journey taken with a god who is on the road together with him. With or without faith, travelling is more important than arriving, the questions are more important than the answers.

The awareness of mortality, that cumbersome co-passenger we reluctantly carry around with us, imparts the need to reach for a higher intensity of life. Life that relentlessly destroys. Life that fades, goes up in smoke and en route stops only at a series of often totally insignificant snapshots, fireflies in eternal darkness. Compassion is a word I do not care for, it is sympathy I approve of. We all count on that in the end, when our time comes, just as we depend on it at every crossroad in our life and relationships.

For all these reasons the weakness of the human condition must instigate resistance, a violent non-assimilation. Better start doing something! Sing, fight, cry, pray, laugh, work and admire. And do travel! Do not accept limits in your head. Make a journey. Go on a quest. Everyone needs anchor points: relational, social, philosophical, professional. Too many uncertainties undermine and deteriorate the quality of life.

> *In a field*
> *I am the absence of field*
> *This is always the case*
> *wherever I am*
>
> *I am what is missing*
> *When I walk I part the air*
> *and always*
> *the air moves in to fill the spaces*
> *where my body's been*
>
> *We all have reasons for moving*
> *I move to keep things whole*
> Mark Strand

The young man or woman embarking upon this journey can count on attacks of internal panic. Sometimes grotesque attacks. A lover of Cohen's first poetry even described the young man she met as, *'a travelling body of pain'*. Leonard Cohen: *'I think that is the ocean in which we are all swimming. We all want to dissolve. We all need that experience of forgetting who we are. I think that is what love is – you forget who you are. Forgetting who you are is such a delicious experience and so frightening that we are in this conflicted predicament. You want it but you really cannot support it. So I think that really what our training, what our culture, our religious institutions, our educational and cultural institutions should be about is preparing the heart for that journey outside of the cage of the ribs.'*

The risk is: you can leave yourself at the mercy of anything. Rimbaud wanted everything, all his life, without any measure. And he wanted it here and now. He had no time to lose, or rather the opposite. Boredom, exaggeration, descending into the hell of lust, drinking and inspiration had to be celebrated as part of the Fine Arts. Rimbaud became the prototype of the man who attacks life: hungry, greedy, horny, incontrovertible. His myth still works. Following the small circle of contemporaries to whom he was the great role model came the Surrealists, in turn followed by the Beat Poets, the Jazz People, the Rockers and the followers of the Gothic Revival.

In his younger years, Cohen, like me, regularly lost his way. Go, go, go, *'go racing in the street'* to say it in the style of Bruce Springsteen. Only idiots are mild towards the young person they used to be. Most hold a false sympathy for their own youth. It was neither exclusively innocent, wonderful, virtuous nor holy. As a youngster one is already a bit of everything: full of promise, absurd, wrong, right. Young guys fill themselves up with every brew that can knock them off this planet, use every sort of dope that scorches their consciousness enough not to leave any permeable feeling. Rebels? *With* or *without* a cause? Definitely rebels incapable of throwing a bomb. Thinkers that invariably see the various aspects of the world, the outer reaches of every enterprise. Holy and rotten at the same time.

Only he who wants to banish adventure and surprise out of his life in advance makes definite choices in his youth. Having enrolled at the prestigious McGill University, Cohen threw himself at a wide range of subjects. Notwithstanding the influence of Professor Louis Dudek and – even more – guest speaker and enfant terrible of Jewish-Canadian poetry, Irving

Layton, he carved out his own road. In so doing he was certainly not slowed by Layton's continually returning question, *'Leonard, are you sure you are doing the wrong thing?'* Personally, I dived with reckless abandon into the full world outside the campuses. The university of life brought me to a myriad of worlds small and large, having to do, vaguely and less vaguely, with literature. Even if writers do not reveal anything and only create more questions to which they owe an answer, it proved impossible not to become an author.

While having all the prerequisites for happiness in those young bud days, you can just as easily claim the right to be deeply unhappy, even against all logic. Who reflects consciously or unconsciously, seldom or never escapes the intense senseless, negative feeling that accompanies life. An oppressive load that can take your psyche apart. Cohen never felt the yearning to put a 'lost paradise' à la Proust up against it. No feather-light hope in his work for him, rather a leaden despair. Yet *'hope is a dream that progresses,'* Aristotle already knew. And so, you continue the journey of your life with intellectual *envergure.*

The Eastern goal of renunciation and asceticism is still faraway in that phase of your development. As a Westerner you almost instinctually choose the road of further exploration. Everyone hopes to come home one day. Alas, as Cohen so bluntly put it in his *Canadien Errant,* you do not have a home any more. At the most you can start in the past and begin your own quest from there. We all have to create our very own point of departure in life. We are all heirs to a birthplace. Being born in Montreal implies that one is part of the history of that city and shares its feeling. In Cohen's youth three separate groups dominated the city on the river: a large francophone population, the English-speaking Canadians and about two percent Jews. Notwithstanding their limited number, the latter group was very much a presence, mainly because of its disproportionately large contribution to art and culture. The big blending together still had to start.

Myself, I have cursed my culturally hushed birthplace Lier more than I praised it. Does that release me from it? Not really. I remain a child from a tiny village in Belgium, that small country in between languages. Contrast it to the immensity of Canada, caught from sea to sea in a highly comparable gentle linguistic stranglehold. Two countries, both afflicted by a sort of lethargy, constantly battling within themselves and marked by a persistent Surrealism. Belgium can present Magritte, while Canada continues to sport *The Progressive Conservatives*, a political party. Belgians filled up half their country in a mad building rush. The large majority of Canadians live on the border with the US, leaving the rest of the country an awesome sea of emptiness where all kinds of flipped-out religious sects established themselves.

Writers pre-eminently lead a sedentary life, but their mind is outspokenly nomadic. Across the directions of the four winds they thread experiences together like a string of beads. Authors do not follow a strict pattern, not even an imaginary line. A detour often is the only way to present itself as plausible, as true. Neither I nor Leonard Cohen remained loyal to our hometown. Cohen took the maxim Canada officially added to the weapon of the country in 1994 – *Desiderantes Mehorem Patriam* (they wish a better fatherland) – quite literally many years before that date. *'Becoming what they call a bohemian was not encouraged by families like my own,'* he says. *'It was most charitably considered a phase the child would grow out of. But in my case... I did not grow out of it. It got worse and worse.'* His reputation would indeed be one of a man constantly on the road, literally or philosophically, as long as the word can travel with him. The hotel room man. Yet he never really said good-bye. He is a bohemian with extraordinary strong roots. Deep inside the desire to go back burned on. Plato already knew the soul turns into a drunk when it touches change.

Luckily, a concept like the constancy of personality does not exist. Visions change, grow, wilt, die off, less influenced by season or temperament than anchored in the mind of each

19

right-thinking person. Authors do not live with their backs turned to the world either. Even a personality turned inward by sheer writer's necessity and a rather reclusive life style will not allow that. Everything is subject to change. Notwithstanding a sizable subsidy and a matching ticket, the young Cohen did not intend to continue travelling when he landed in London to write his first novel there in the fall of 1959. The young Jew only chose to travel on because he could not get used to the English climate. London, paradigm rather than synonym of grey, was unbearable. A Burberry raincoat and a portable typewriter, both hardened against all types of weather, were Cohen's only real conquests there. A city so tame, so passive, so cast down and impervious to any form of poetry or jazz, could never be sincerely swinging.

And thus Leonard Cohen travelled on. Searching for his own particular space in the Diaspora. He did not choose pomp and circumstance, nor glitter. Not Vienna, for instance, but the sober, barren and unexploited Greek island of Hydra. Isolated and highly uncomfortable at the time of Cohen's arrival, the high romantic content that this episode of his life would later be ascribed is not warranted in the least. He truly is at the far edge of the world. Here, on this small, inhospitable island with less than 2000 inhabitants, squeezed between the Gulf of Argolis and the Gulf of Aegina, between the Aegean and the Cretan Sea, Cohen would establish himself. Hydra, a living cemetery in comparison to Montreal, offered him ideal circumstances to order his thoughts in almost complete isolation and at an affordable price.

George Johnston and Charmian Clift, Australian journalists, had preceded him. In her book *Peel Me a Lotus*, Clift reported their struggle to survive on the rocky island, together with their two small children. When Cohen arrived there, the Johnston book *Closer to the Sun* had just appeared, and with it the first fissures in their marriage. The duo helped the newcomer settle in. Other writers, musicians and painters followed. By the mid-sixties, when the Johnstons left, a small group of artists lived almost continuously under the never balmy sun and the heavily distorted beauty of Hydra. Cohen was neither a leader nor a follower. From his house, 'a thousand steps' above the charming small harbor, he was part of the clockwork, the invariable nature of island life. The sound of the church bells, the boat with produce, arriving at ten sharp, street cats stopping by his terrace, the talking shopkeepers and the hooves of the easy-going carrier donkeys clickety-clacking on the cobblestones. All this proved he belonged, that he too had his regular place in the café at the brittle, painful moment when days draw to a close. Rituals a person only achieves when he manages to temporarily stop the din in his head. With the same great persistence as the natural elements surrounding him, Cohen worked at his task. On Hydra he wrote some of his best texts.

Smaller, more limited, I escaped my provincial nest. From a place at the outskirts of the city I started my Odyssey in the margin of time, looking for keys. Applying myself to a sensitive way of writing in the first place. Cohen's work having helped him to find his singularity, the reconstructions I created in turn defined my route. Ever clearer and more emphatically, I saw the under-lying connections. Structures and influences slowly gave up their secrets and pointed to the only road possible. After a while there is this unfathomable certainty. Then you feel, you know: I am beginning to fit into this skin.

Real life starts. Indolent in the beginning, but gaining ground fast. The outside world is exactly that: outside your world. As thrilling as the cardiogram of a deceased person, the forever ugly noon light barely disturbing. A situation that is intense enough, can overthrow mental frameworks in a minimum of time. You live on your own cloud, with its fixed location and its unchangeable times, customs and habits.

Astonishing maybe, this almost obsessive yearning of free spirits for strict schedules. Singer-poet Cohen even advocates an outspoken iron fist approach as the ideal antidote for every possible form of anarchy. Dreamers are immediately and definitely excluded. Their attitude, their reality, is one that, according to Cohen, makes for lack of control. Paul Valéry wrote: *'Out of the greatest discipline grows the greatest wisdom.'* Authors like us have to add to this, nolens volens, *'out of personal necessity and life preservation.'* Cohen even takes it one step further: *'I myself like the sense of order that is associated with military training. I'm not talking about warfare. I'm talking about the kind of uncompromising training that is necessary to open the heart to the fact that it is not alone.'*

Authenticity and sincerity remain the motive. Avoid ways out, sidetracks or short cuts. Opt consciously and out of free will for an, at times, hated dead-or-do discipline. The long search to conceive and fulfil a strictly personal path. Time, space and the reality in which you move around apparently are no more than a backdrop. Much more important is the synthesis that can be arrived at, the balance between the masses and the individual. In his *Siddhartha*, the bible of those who search, Herman Hesse has suggested that integration in the surrounding world is not the issue. Rather, the coinciding of your vision with a vague ideal of 'I' is. Therein lies liberation, the autonomy in which all difficulties and contradictions of life can be solved. Or to quote Hegel: *'Freedom is to be in possession of oneself.'*

Alas, long-lasting immobility is not granted to a young, economically dependent author. Leonard Cohen didn't escape the laws of economics either. Hydra became a launching pad rather than a home. If his journeys were originally undertaken as part of books under construction, he later went on the road again with a totally new goal: to turn the financial tide. His *Beautiful Losers*, which broke new ground and received magnificent reviews, failed to succeed on the monetary front. Disappointed in the harvest of his talents, Cohen decided on a radical change of course. He envisioned that his poetry might sell as country songs. Thus Nashville became his destination. On his way there, Cohen walked into an ambush: the Chelsea Hotel, New York City. The street sang, the entrance hall spoke, the rooms breathed modern cultural history. Everybody who was someone in the alternative folk-and-pop scene passed or hung out there in the mid-sixties.

Leonard Cohen was lucky, extremely lucky. Not only did he manage to remain on the right side of madness, but from the Chelsea he would break through commercially – worldwide – as a songwriter and singer. Cohen, looking back: *'It was dangerous to accept a potato chip at a cocktail party then. I speak literally. It could be sprinkled with acid. I went to somebody's room who was having a cocktail party, had a few chips, and four days later was still trying to find my room.'*

Fortunately, the enormous success that came his way during that period did not cloud Cohen's critical judgment. He ripped the so oftenglorified sixties to pieces. *'Everybody went for the money. Everybody. The thing died out very, very quickly. The merchants took over. Evidence that nothing was really happening accumulated.'* Even more destructively, the singer-songwriter lashed out at the poseurs who deliberately emulated the spirit of the time. Leonard Cohen: *'I do not have to have a song called "Give Peace a Chance". I could write a song about conflict and, if I sang it in a peaceful way, then it would have the same message. I do not like these slogan writers.'*

Me, after six years of heavy toll, I could wallow in the attention of the press and audiences for the first time. An experience: let's leave it at that. Way more important was the content of that first publication. Something that still resounds today, thanks to several updated re-editions of my firstborn. More importantly, readers who, over the years, took the trouble to go through the work thoroughly, often told how honest and unbiased my conclusions seemed to them. Only logical in my eyes, given that I, like Cohen, always clung to that one single intransigent goal: report the truth, or come as close to it as one is ever likely to get.

Speaking about modern popular music the know-it-alls and culture popes are countless. *'The maestro says it's Mozart, but it sounds like bubblegum,'* Leonard Cohen sings. Trash is too often promoted as great art. And the other way around this axiom works just as well. Elvis Presley was assailed by self-respecting journalists in 1956 when he and he alone turned the music world upside down. Ten years later, Leonard Cohen was also run into the ground. Cohen: '*Remember the way that a lot of rock and roll was greeted by the authorities and the musicologists and even the hip people. And when people were putting me down as being one thing or another, it was not the guy in the subway. He did not know about me. It was the hip people, writing the columns in the hip newspapers, college papers, music papers.*' The same people, in other words, who ascribe the original, innovating role to that self-declared '*Working Class Hero*'. The singer-composer/large landowner behind '*Give Peace a Chance*' and his group, privileged heirs of the biggest musical revolution of the last century. Factually wrong? In reality and in figures? No problem! They go on promoting the idea. For a writer to whom authenticity and honesty are at stake a challenge to take on. Cohen: '*It is very difficult to see what the verdict is going to be about a piece of work. And the thing that really makes it an interesting game is that each generation revises the game, and decides on what is poetry and song for itself, often rejecting the very carefully considered verdicts of the previous generations.*' Music begins where words end.

*You*
*sun and moon*
*I*
*bathing in your rays*

That first period of writing is long gone. Travelling and roaming, literally more focused. Yet what is this often-praised passion worth? Who or what feeds it? Permanently? Or for a very short while? The answers to these questions influence our perception of our existence more than we can imagine. Leonard Cohen, as well as your servant, spent the early writing years in a self-created world that we had ordered ourselves. But even though the strict and binding rules were entirely in function of writing, they did not determine everything. The role of our respective partners in life was too important for that. Often they broke through the shield of the writer, stole us from our creation, disrupted the image we had in mind, claimed us.

24

As young authors we stumbled over that difference between reality and perception. Like a shadow it followed us, day in, day out, from sunrise to sunset. Eventually the details of our shabby honeymoon no longer mattered. In spite of all secondary reasons, the ultimate realization is that our only true marriage is to our self, to our ideals. The blow that dealing with the disintegration of a self-constructed world delivers to your doorstep is hard to handle. The worst reproaches being hurled at you; having to admit silently to the biggest shortcomings, it is sheer horror. And still, still all of that is not as hard to risk as the stigma of being a renegade. You do not forfeit your task in life. And so a new search was in order. For him. For me. The singer-poet did not want to hear it said or even suggested that he faced the world like a man. He too failed, cracked up, broke. A Cohen-motto could be: In life you have to be able to leave things behind. Clear the deck, let it be, abandon and start anew. Quite a challenge for someone like me, stuck knee-deep in the remnants of a very conservative upbringing, my father's mark on the soul.

Cohen's new place was Tennessee. He rented a withered farm, inland and totally desolate, from songwriter Boudleaux Bryant. His spirit was in ruins, a wasteland. Mentally he collapsed to a point from which many do not return. Myself, I got no farther than Antwerp, the closest big city, winding up on the fringe of it pretty quickly, totally emasculated. Subconsciously I found myself in Alexandria, symbol of lost knowledge, the impossibility to know, to master. Books that could change lives just disappeared.

In some indistinct way, the things that must happen do indeed come to pass. New destinations, new roads, new writings. While Cohen maintained his house on Hydra as a refuge and his office in LA for business, I began from a similar position, building my own functional hideout and workspace. It was not a matter of example or imitation. The subconscious, fed by experience, afraid of repetition and stimulated by a relentless quest for security, serves as a guide. For Leonard Cohen as well as for myself, our rise and fall, however different, in the end became the instrument of a renewed acquaintance with ourselves. It would help us to get closer to the nucleus, to our inevitable task and the ultimate consequence thereof, equally unavoidable for everyone in this life: the truth. Sooner or later, everybody has to look the truth, his or her truth, in the eye. Leonard Cohen: *'We are drawn to the truth. We are drawn to the truth when we hear it and when we see it. We are hungry for the truth. We are always surprised because the truth manifests itself in so many different ways and in so many different forms. You can hear it from your friend, from your wife, from your children. You can hear it for a moment in a song on the radio. It is so precious when you hear it that you are immediately drawn to it. So I tend to be wary of confining this expression of truth to one kind of activity. Millions of people go to church and receive real sustenance from the liturgy, from the religious situation in their communities. I do not think it serves anything to diminish human effort in any category. So I could never take a position about where the truth manifests more clearly, more beautifully. The fact is that we are all embraced by the truth continually and sometimes we know it and sometimes we do not.'*

> *The birds they sang*
> *at the break of day*
> *Start again*
> *I heard them say*
> *Don't dwell*
> *on what has passed away*
> *or what is yet to be*
> *Ring the bells that still can ring*
> *Forget your perfect offering*
> *There is a crack in everything*
> *That's how the light gets in*
> Leonard Cohen

Chapter 4

EVEN DAMNATION IS POISONED WITH RAINBOWS

*I am not life,*
*I am not death*
*I am not slave or free*
Leonard Cohen

The slices of life that have been dealt with bring us back to our soul, with the recognition of our limitations. The tension between longing and resignation, between chasing dreams and making cold compromises may have lessened. The inwardly turned character that has survived a difficult background is able to open up again, better than ever even. The sure knowledge of the paths you have walked drives you irrevocably towards your possibilities. No irremovable mass of calluses, no unlimited shortcomings, not even your very own stupidity can stop that.

Wittgenstein estimated that we will never totally grasp certain things and that it is better to keep one's silence about those. Goethe was wise enough to impress upon us that we should pay attention to *'the green meadow'*, that which makes life worth living for each of us, while Louis-Ferdinand Céline as grandmaster of negativity kept preaching the futility of life. Beautiful, stylized visions. In sharp contrast to Cohen's decades-old reputation, this *'man of ink black lack of illusions and gloominess'*, the *'doom-monger pur sang'* which he is considered to be, offers a vision that is much closer to what is authentic and real.

Leonard Cohen: *'It is the notion that there is no perfection. That this is a broken world, and we live with broken hearts and broken lives but still that is no alibi for anything.'* Only from that vantage point can you go on walking among the ruins.

The absurd imperfection of life is inevitable. The sign of Cain marks us all. Rich or poor, in spite of the differences in well-being and privileges, we have all been dealt that same card. Oscar Wilde already knew that in a society like ours, in which property brings immense distinction, social position, honor, respect, titles and other advantages, the naturally ambitious human being makes it his goal to enlarge his personal property. Sorrow, misery and downfall slap the loser of the game as a cold, wet rag in the face. He or she loses all certainties, conviction and self-confidence. Adversity and defeat harden a man, they say. As long as that man does not break down completely. It is not exceptional to think in a moment of an extraordinary ordeal that your best days are over, your future has had its best time. Unnecessary to convince us of that.

Leonard Cohen: *'A pessimist is somebody who is waiting for the rain. Me, I'm already wet. I do not wait for the rain to fall. We are in the catastrophe. There's no point in waiting for it. Everybody knows it. The evidence accumulates that ours is not an entirely happy undertaking. The amount of suffering that one sees and hears about is shattering. The only comfort in the matter is Thy Will Be Done. To whatever degree you want to establish that as a principle in your life: the notion that it is unfolding according to a mechanism that you cannot possibly penetrate. Accept it. Or surrender.'*

Whatever the case, people fight for the crumbs of the bread of charity. Life is our beginning and end, over the bounds of time and space. And we cannot always discover logic, or the humanity we so cultivate, in what that life respects or does not respect. Think of the countless genocides, or the horrible way we still treat our defenseless fellow earthlings, the animals. A gross parallel? A boost of our contemporary action group culture? Just the same you could start a theological discussion about the subject. Buddhists, in contrast to Christians for instance, believe in respect for all life. Rather, the aim should be to keep you alert. Your eyes have to go on sending pain signals to your brain, even if they have seen too many truths.

28

The risks of getting accustomed to all this is not a minor one, argued ace writer Marguerite Yourcenar when she stated that nobody, not even the soldiers who were charged with the convoys, would have tolerated the fully loaded train carriages in 1940–1945 if we had not accepted for generations to see animals suffocate in animals carts.

*We've been around*
*We fought, we fly*
*We mostly fall*
*We mostly run*
*And every now and then we try*
*to mend the damage that we've done*
Leonard Cohen

Sense of guilt. The heavy word is out. As if it is not bad enough that we have to live with our self and our weaknesses we also have the ability to morally weigh aberrations in our behavior and that of others. Although, who today still has a guilty conscience? Day by day we seem better trained to find cover for ourselves. *'That is the way I am,'* is the fashionable statement. There is something to be said for it. When you wake up, you cannot really choose who you would want to be that day. You are stuck with your own self, like it or not. An option you do have, in all you do, is the unavoidable choice between Apollo and Dionysus, between mind, ratio, and celebration, pleasure. In the end, that fact will push you towards guilt again, guaranteed. Terrible? Not really. Leonard Cohen calls feelings of guilt *'an essential part of the human mind'* and considers it a big mistake to have them removed by medication or other means. *'I think guilt is an excellent indication of the fact that you are doing something wrong, or that you have done something wrong. It should be studied and embraced and understood and blessed.'* As a conscious human being you cannot and should not run away from your own. A right-minded person is a soul searcher.

The art is to take note, without wallowing in our human impotence. Emancipated as we are, we barely get across the threshold of observation. Ridiculous hedonists are we, puny mythomaniacs, fighting in vain against our insignificance. Only out of that awareness, that 'Zen' that puts everything into perspective, can we begin to reconstruct our crumbling existence into a working totality and live in serene harmony with our surroundings and our fellow earthlings. Call it 'Thy Will be Done' or define it as a pure Lucebertian awareness of our role in the universe. It is our only solace. Leonard Cohen: *'The light is the capacity to reconcile your experience, your sorrow, with every day that dawns. It is that understanding, which is beyond significance or meaning, that allows you to live a life and embrace the disasters and sorrows and joys that are our common lot. But it is only with the recognition that there is a crack in everything. All other visions are doomed to irretrievable gloom.'*

Looking in the mirror no longer is looking into an abyss. For the second time you claim the leading part in your own small tragedy. After all you become human by entering the world as an individual. In doing so your own identity risks being partially determined by others. Are you weighed down by all the conventions imposed on you? Or not? It certainly is warmer and safer within the group than outside it. And of course, there is fear.

Of one's own shortcomings, of violence, of death. Farewell then to the individual? Not in the name of this author, not in the name of Leonard Cohen. Our craving for freedom is unquestioned. Yet we both agree that the idea of a Messiah is very attractive. Believing in brotherhood, in a society that is compassionate, in people living for more than themselves. Our position is one of outspoken humanism. At the end of the day you should be able to still believe in people. Continue to resist the supremacy of money, institutions and religions. As a person you have to be able to go on functioning autonomously, freed of the dominant structures.

It sometimes gives you the feeling that you are rubbing against reality without ever really grasping it. If you fail to get a grip on reality, you try to cleanse yourself spiritually. No thinking of ideologies, rituals or preferences for a moment. No thinking at all. Go back to the source. Live very intensely as an empty shell, without content and hollow, averse to the summoned sounds that speak of adventure, nihilism or lamentation. Open up the room in which all your longings and fears are hidden. Soon you will be liberated from the human wish to symbolically connect future and present, death and life, and to narrow your existence to a prison with two gates. It does not revolve around death or life at all, but around the intensity with which you live. Leonard Cohen: *'Everyone comes to a point when they have to find value in their life, when one must find metaphors to explain the significance of one's own life. Whether it is through charity, meditation, therapy or financial enrichment; no matter what activity one chooses the intention is the same: to find a metaphor for the profound hunger to be significant in some way. Religious traditions fill that need but if it cannot or does not for some people, other metaphors will emerge. Everyone continuously examines, fights and corrects his metaphors. It is not something that is definite or acquired; it is an endless activity. One continuously revises it in one's own way.'* Most logically, the bard refuses to push forward a unified goal of life. *'To know our purpose or the significance of our existence is not within our reach. Our objective, if there is one, is to relax our search for meaning, because it is not attainable.'* Personally, I would like to propagate a contained striving for purity and authenticity. Follow your drives and enjoy. Have others enjoy, without harming yourself or other beings. Be skeptical towards shining paths, charismatic leaders, publicity, hype or fashion trends. Be on your guard against every mass. Living consciously is living against better judgment. As, even when the struggle seems hopeless, that inner struggle still has to be waged. Resistance does not start with big words, but with small deeds.

> *And summoned now to deal*
> *With your invincible defeat*
> *You live your life as if it's real*
> *A thousand kisses deep*
> Leonard Cohen

Nobody controls his own life. If that were the case, every life would look different. Almost everybody would immediately implement needed and sometimes drastic adaptations. Understanding that we are not in control is the first token of our irrevocable awakening.

Cohen: *'After that, you have to understand that you have to live on as if your life is real, as if you are the director and as if your choices have got consequences that are predictable. Life is to choose and therefore we have to carry on making these choices as if they are real choices that we can control. The deeper understanding is that you do not run the show, but live your life 'a thousand kisses deep', and by that phrase I mean that you have to accept the mystery and surrender to it. And not even that is under your control. Before you actually experience the surrender, you do not even know the shape of it.'* Thus the author who once described an imprint in the snow, a trace of the past presence of a person as his *'favorite game'*, has landed on his pet subject: surrender. Better than most Cohen knows that our heart, this visceral wonder, is forever spewing emotions, eternal stumbling blocks. Seamless, he adds the insight that you can only really enjoy when you succeed in disappearing, in losing your-self in the moment. Leonard Cohen: *'When one does not exist then one can enjoy what is received. For example, when you embrace your children or your beloved, or when you drink a cold glass of water. When you are thirsty, you dissolve in the cold water, in the sweet hug of your child and you forget yourself. That is a very refreshing occasion, and it is paradise: there is no you. But you resurrect immediately. If you are lucky, you resurrect with the residue of the experience.'*

The messy reality. For a moment you do not know for sure whether you are still there. Then follows chastened consolation. The true perfection of man does not lie in what he owns, but in what he is, in what he could be. According to Roger Walsh, professor in psychiatry, philosophy and anthropology, the words asceticism, love, virtuousness, concentration, consciousness, wisdom and servitude are keywords of what he has dubbed 'the seven paths to the heart and mind'. Though the academic seemingly pulls a handful of concepts out of the wealth of notions of the different world religions, this series of words does bring us close to our small personal truth. You stand up as a free person, ready to open and surrender your heart.

Chapter 5

GENESIS

Everybody is born. In that respect all are equal. Yet the future does not hold the same wide-open opportunities for everyone. For that, the family you are born into is too determining. The typical Jewish view of the family as a clan, around which the whole world revolves, was central in young Leonard Cohen's life. A given that was cast in stone. Leonard was not born into just any family. The Cohens, Kohanim, representatives of a select group of high priests from Israel, were entrusted heavy responsibilities in the matter of the Tradition-with-a-capital.

Lyon Cohen, son of a Lithuanian-born Jew who immigrated to Canada soon after its founding and was the head of the largest garment company in the country. Moreover, he was the youngest chairperson ever of the most prominent synagogue in Canada and vice-chairman of the first Zionist organization in that immense country. As if all that was not enough, he also founded the first English language Jewish newspaper in North America. Nathan B. Cohen, son of Lyon, was injured as a lieutenant during World War I, with permanent, serious health problems as a consequence. Nathan married Masha, eighteen years younger, the daughter of Rabbi Klinitsky-Klein. The rabbi, who like his father and granddad had fulfilled an important task maintaining the Jewish teachings in Poland by publishing influential theological writings, had fled to Canada in 1923. There he developed a close bond with his old pen pal Lyon Cohen. That their children found each other was no coincidence. After daughter Esther, their first and only son came into the world: Leonard, the successor.

Far more modest expectations accompanied my first steps into this world. The combination of a clever and hardworking, always straight father, betrayed in his naïveté by a promiscuity-loving beauty, did not exactly predict a lot of good. Neither did the fatalism with which his predecessor had seen his life reduced to a second-string role through an unforeseen mix of circumstances.

Ready for the *comédie humaine* which awaits each one of us, the youth of a child growing up in a well-to-do family runs along different paths. Cohen, a youngster in the days of WW II, saw much of the burning world pass him and his family by. The children lived with their parents on a beautiful estate and were served by a maid, a nanny and a chauffeur-cum-gardener. Every time Nathan stayed home sick, which was a recurrent event, Masha took care of him. Through this, the children became more influenced than planned by their Irish, Catholic nanny. For Leonard Cohen the first opening to a different faith from the Jewish religion in which he was being raised. Cohen: *'We had strong religious practices and beliefs. Religion structured our life. My parents did not make a big deal out of it, they were not fanatics. It was mentioned no more than a fish mentions the presence of water. We celebrated the Sabbath every Friday night. We lit candles, which I still do. We said prayers, we went to the synagogue Saturday morning, to Sunday school, to Hebrew school three times a week. All this in conjunction with a normal Canadian education.'*

Even if it sounds a bit strange today, young Cohen was not absorbed by religion, nor by the word or the language of it all. He did feel lucky that his parents never presented to him the Supreme Being as a strict, demanding God, something Cohen to this day classifies as *'an act of great compassion'*. As soon as Leonard was old enough to speak, he was educated at home, in the classroom, and in Hebrew school, in the words of the *shema*, the confession of faith of Judaism, originated on Mount Sinai in direct contact between Yahweh and Moses. Growing up, he learned more and more words, until he could fully recite the Jewish creed. It became part of his deeper consciousness. Following the *Mishnah* came the second phase of his Jewish upbringing: Leonard's *bar mitzvah*. Only the circumcision is a more important event in the life of a young male Jew.

Traditions. They exist to open your road to the future. Often, they show you where to go, what to do. With them come pettiness and big ideals, the narrow-mindedness and warmth that are part of it and which you will not let go, same as they refuse to let go of you. If you manage not to be blinded by the emotion called past, it is one of the first conclusions you'll come to. My kind and well-intentioned grandmother did her best to replace my absent mother. Alas, the good soul also fed me a fair portion of highly traditional insights into the Lord and his work. In contrast to Cohen, the language did move me; it was the content itself that failed to leave much of an imprint on my soul. The Saviour, as he was offered to me, appeared much too tainted with the long-outlived concepts of guilt and punishment.

Strange, is it not, how casually a child manages to shrug off a great deficiency? Leonard's father seemed but a passing shade in his existence, more alive in the filmed images than in the imagination of his son that was not put on celluloid. Only when he passed away – when Leonard was nine – did pain cut through the young heart. Hailing from a disrupted family, I never had the feeling that my homely nest lacked any of the security, safety or completeness that a child can expect. At most, my young life was overshadowed at some unexpected, unannounced times by the threat of my mother's unspoken deeds.

With some ill-will, both of us could be reproached as being unhappy Sunday's children. Leonard grew up in wealth. I flitted through an almost too carefree youth. And yet, all too often you feel you are losing at moments of success. During childhood you suddenly live that blessed and cursed moment when for the first time you understand things that are inconceivable. You know how it feels when trusted ground starts sliding. People who are important in your life die. The recognition does not bring merriment. Grown up, before you know what that word means. A boy, a lad still, acknowledging That one can die at any given time that still manages to keep his cool. It is a gift for life. I do not wish it on anybody, but understanding so much at once, recognizing the complexity, the ambiguity and cruelty of life and achieving a clear, empirical view, it is a spiritual gift. He or she who experiences it, emerges a stronger person.

What follows is an enormous discrepancy between your unbridled ambition and the scantiness of your experiences. What experience in life does a person need as an incentive to create, to write? A confrontation with death? Why else does Cohen write down a message, roll it in a bowtie in order to hide it meticulously in the cold January soil? Because he didn't know his father well enough? Because he felt short-changed by him? Or simply because being a Jew he grew up with words? Because the history of his people makes it clear that the word in itself is not sufficient, yet essential in tradition? He and I, we both fail to give a direct answer.

The pure, clarified poetry of Federico Garcia Lorca, in which he uses surrealist and at the same time romantic and sensitive images, is an eye opener for the young Leonard Cohen. His Spanish grain will not be standing in the plain. Lorca's work teaches him that images too beautiful for literality can work, can even be popular. A path opens. Years later Cohen himself will be a source where many come to drink. To me, his work helped in the same degree as Lorca's creations once helped him. A lift, indispensable in order to leave behind the world from which you came.

The years of one's youth. Many use them during their life as a kind of alibi or a trump card. But whether you are favorably disposed to Eastern or Western religion, whether you speak about 'waking up' or being 'born again', it is not the metaphor but the fact itself that is important. Everyone should reach that point. Only then can your very own journey begin, free of excess baggage and with an open mind. The absurdity of your experiencescan then span your whole existence and being. A lot you will take with you everywhere you go; yet endlessly more you leave behind. Again, and again you define and redefine your position and map your totally unique route.

Chapter 6

A ROSE IN YOUR TEA

*For the innermost decision*
*That we cannot but obey*
*For what's left of our religion*
*I lift my voice and pray*
Leonard Cohen

It is difficult not to feel aversion to religion when you see what it does to people: how unhappy many became with themselves because of it and how that distanced them from others. Slick zealots build their perfidious rhetoric directly or indirectly on resentment living under the skin and they shamelessly claim to be absolutely right, their religion being the only true one. Even if their credibility is in a deplorable state, from under their layer of fast fading glory they go on ruling unabashed.

Regarded objectively, religion carries a very unpleasant odor. Faith, along with the love of or for God, for believers is a different matter. The exclusive way in which faith is appropriated and lived may be reprehensible. Years ago, Marguerite Yourcenar already understood that the deception lies not in the dogmas, the rites or legends. These can be perfectly admirable, even healthy for the human psyche. The deceit is in the presumptuous claims that the representatives of faith propagate, as if they are the only ones to have a direct connection to God. A true believer does not demand exclusivity. Each large religion confirms other religions, just as a strong culture confirms other cultures or a big nation respects other nations.

Instead of being out of fashion until the end of time and resigned to its existence as a richly compensated but purely decorative function, religion could be – and possibly should be – that one precious pearl, the possession of which justifies the sacrifice of all we own on earth. Should not the core of belief revolve around freedom? Serve to uplift the spirit? The wealth of all life experiences? And is the issue today not much more utility and gain than values or possibilities to improve the world? One rarely speaks about religion, because religion is dangerous. Believing touches the deepest of a being, of its soul. Many understand that, and feel it that way. The places of worship may be emptying rapidly, faith – in all its forms – lives. An impressive number of sub-religions recognize this and have a full bazaar of ideologies for sale. Their leaders explicitly capitalize on a feeling of exclusivity, not with the intention to come together in a deeper experience of faith nor to lend a helping hand. Their goal is sheer self-enrichment. Which brings us nothing new. Sophists have been part of the package for centuries. Their cult-religions have always existed. Well thought out or totally ridiculous, 'with the beauty of the word' or based on other sentiments they offer many a form of spiritual interpretation and meaning against a variable price.

One swears by the seriousness and width of the biblical myths in which feelings are elevated to archetypes, to images for eternity. Another goes for religious fundamentalism that sacrifices the personal freedom of the individual to an abstract collective happiness. There is a light in everything; we mentioned it. From the Chlysts to the Baghwan, from God to Yahweh. *Vox populi, vox dei*. The Voice of God, capitalized, may be law, *'the truth has to dawn slowly so that it does not blind,'* poet Emily Dickinson has indicated.

Like no other, Leonard Cohen uses mystic parables to explain the facts of life on different levels. He deals with the hallowed and the secular, what is human and what is godly. Moreover, he succeeds in showing what is heavenly by promoting what is of this earth. Cohen summarizes his vision on the role of faith in our life as follows: *'Religions are among the great organizing principles of humanity. It seems to me they matter too much and not enough.'* The old master will not get caught holding on to strict ethical or moral points of view. For that his awareness is too acute that he – an example to many – is too much of an apprentice himself. Cohen continuous to search. His bond with *'The Nameless and The Name'* has been strong since his childhood days, but where his name originally stood for priest, the Latin translation of Cohen is *Pontifex*, bridge. Leonard Cohen indeed builds bridges between religions. Two hearts instead of two triangles did not accidentally form the Star of David on the cover of his poetry book and psalm collection *Book of Mercy*. The heart sees better than the eye, teaches the rabbi. It is better to break open one's faith than to follow it loyally.

I myself come from a linguistic area in which an eminence like Reve exemplified that religion does not, by definition, need to be associated with narrow-minded ideas burning with hell and damnation. The subject can also be dealt with in an attractive, penetrating and even spirited way, whether you speak solemnly about that one indivisible teaching or whether for you personally Bibles, Torahs and Korans are all, without distinction, apocryphal history. Spinoza was still considered a rebel when he negated the godly origin of the Torah and thus robbed it of its legitimacy. Newton and the philosopher Locke, later Voltaire, Diderot and Rousseau put reason first as guide, renounced magic and superstition and made Enlightenment viable.

Freethinking was a fact. One can ask the question why the Age of Reason came about in Holland with the Reformed Church, while in those parts of the world where Catholicism, Islam or Judaism dominated it never fully took flight. Could it be because the sense of reason is limited? Reason is a working method, a means to go through life. Never can it be a goal in itself. Then humans have nothing left but a vulnerable veneer of individuality amidst a cynical, cold secular society. The true liberal will postulate that we will overcome even that. Alas, living autonomously, interpreting our existence in a joyful and imaginative manner, is something that millions of people completely fail to master. They all take refuge in overfilled agendas and obsessive pleasure, while desperately longing for more spiritual depth. The number of books trying to compensate for the disappearance of the religious and secular authorities for these people is truly ridiculous.

To most citizens the alternatives offered by the conservatives, gurus and freethinkers are hardly believable, not applicable and/or not true enough. Cohen's work does contain this authenticity even though it as well features morality or belief. The art of living, looking for the task of our life, is a concept that has played a major role in the philosophy of Friedrich Nietzsche.

As a human you are given a task, and that is not to make as much money as possible or set some kind of record. Your human task is to stand in life well-balanced. To live with a good attitude, with a personality that is firm enough to look its own weaknesses squarely in the eye. To use suffering as a moral criterion to meet the world.

What is life about at this moment? How far have we evolved in understanding it? How do we deal with incomprehension? And how do we deal with life in adversity, when it is stripped of its enchantment, demythologized, senseless and aim- less?

The assumption that there is no deity who manages this world of ours, that there exists no coherent creation, and that humanity is at the mercy of an unfathomable chaos of which it is part, is a vision that a lot of people cannot accept without a sturdy framework, without order. So much we know. Therefore, you would better think it all through thoroughly, possibly assume a higher something that has a lofty moral goal in mind for us.

That keeps it all under control. As Pavese noted in his diary centuries ago: *'The art of living is the art of believing lies.'* It begs the question whether what you create or stage for yourself is by definition non-existent. The angels may sneak a peek, when the devil leaves his porch light on. A romantic image. Do you believe it, or do you just use it?

*Was looking at the crucifix*
*Got something in my eye*
*A light that doesn't need to live*
*and doesn't need to die*
*What's written in the Book of Love*
*is strangely incomplete*
*'til witnessed here in time*
*and blood*
*a thousand kisses deep*
Leonard Cohen

The grandson of Baal-Shem-Tov, the founding father of Chassidism, tells in one of his enumerable sagas how one of his best students suddenly does not show up or keep in touch. The rabbi goes and looks up the young man and tells him: *'I know what is wrong.'* The young man reacts hesitantly, apologetic: *'I have studied hard these last weeks and meditated, Master, and suddenly all my certainties were gone. I do not know anything anymore and I doubt everything. I could not come to you or to anybody. I became very unhappy because of it.'*

To this the rabbi replies: *'I told you I know what is troubling you! Without knowing you have walked through the fiftieth gate. The first forty-nine you have opened. Always you found a riddle and always you solved it. Behind every solved dilemma you stood in front of another gate and another question of life. Forty-nine times. Then you entered the fiftieth gate. It opened and you found there The Question, the one nobody can answer, because when you have answered The Question, there are no choices any more. You are no longer free. If you dare to address that question, you are lost.'*

*'But, do I have to return to the beginning and follow another path then?'*

*'Not at all, because without realizing it you already walked through the fiftieth gate.'*

That specific question is of course if there is a God, and if so, what he looks like. A variation of the story known also in Western culture tells how the Jews fleeing from Egypt wandered for forty-nine days through a desolate landscape on their way to the Promised Land. On the fiftieth day Yahweh manifested himself to them with a message of forgiveness and recovery. If one could know for certain that God exists and how he looks, then – so say the Chassidim – you lose your human freedom, your possibility to choose. And thus you lose your very humanity.

As the first-born son of a first-born son, Leonard Norman Cohen, Elieser – God is my Help – with his Hebrew name, was predestined to consecrate himself to the study of the Torah. The Kohanim/Cohens represented an important role model and thus becoming a rabbi was an option. Moreover, given the fact that a Jewish priest is not an official of a daily accessible temple, such a choice would not stand in the way of a leading function in the family business. The rabbis who wrote the Talmud erased the idea of a temple religion from their sacred writings centuries ago. They did, however, keep the memory of the destroyed Temple by proclaiming every pious household to be a temple, which explains the origin of the strict laws of the orthodox Jews. Herein is clearly delineated what is kosher in the home and what is not.

Cohen in other words was predestined to become a spokesperson of Yahweh. As a free spirit, he studied all he was supposed to study and then some. Regardless of the measure of difficulty, the sacrifice and the suffering that this freedom of mind cost, he maintained a critical eye. For him the Talmud was not just 365 prohibitions (one for every day) and 248 commandments (one for every articulation of the human body), just as the holy books of the Torah and the 613 prescriptions contained in them do not stand on their own. He who does not listen but reads, finds more than enough arguments to prove zealous windbags, without hesitation, that there is not only written what they contend. Neither faith, nor its interpretation should ever be stifling for the one introduced to it. From that angle it became possible for Cohen to look for his own spiritual path. '*Happy is the one who knows his place and takes off from there,'* says the Talmud. The three most important pillars of Judaism: the Torah (the first part of the Old Testament), *avodah* (prayer) and *Gemilus Hasidim* (charity) will continue to be part of Leonard Cohen's work and convictions throughout life.

> *May everyone live*
> *And may everyone die*
> *Hello, my love*
> *And my love, Goodbye*
> Leonard Cohen

Whereas in the *Kabbalah*, the mystic Jewish teaching, the heart stands for beauty and the Talmud emphasizes *'God wants the heart, prayer supports the heart,'* Tibetan Buddhism sees the heart as equal to wisdom. Both religions conceive the body and the mind as polar and even components of existence. Cohen's step in the direction of Zen Buddhism would not be a transition, the technique of the 'koan' being deeply rooted in his Chassidic tradition. The rabbi told his pupil a difficult story that did not give answers but incited further thinking, exceeding the limits of the obvious and rational. In *Beautiful Losers* Cohen already demonstrated the singularity of the koan: holiness through sexual satisfaction, getting to know your partner spiritually by knowing him or her physically, a concept that comes together in Zen Buddhism and in Jewish theology refuting the age-old claim of Catholicism and other religions that sexual life should be anything but holy. In the heart of the sixties it was a position that was gladly embraced, albeit for the wrong reasons. The author's entreaty in his roman à clef, wishing to warn for gurus, methods, teachers or lies, fell on deaf ears in a time of relationships without content or depth, with youngsters who considered themselves to be morally superior. To them *Beautiful Losers* was nothing more than the umpteenth instigation to free sex.

Many in that damned decade started searching, but there

were no ready-made solutions to be found. Drug use only intensified the urge. Life became hard. Sunk to the bottom of his personal distress, Leonard Cohen, too, seemed a possible victim. When he met Joshu Sasaki Roshi at his Zen Buddhist monastery on Mount Baldy in the San Gabriel Mountains near Los Angeles for the first time, he was mentally weak and very vulnerable.

Leonard Cohen: *'When the level of suffering in any individual reaches a certain point and he cannot deal with his own discomfort, then he is going to look for some kind of solution. I do not think any religious quest is begun with a sense of luxury. A serious religious examination is not undertaken unless the being is broken with suffering, either physical or psychic. You are being creamed some- how by the world. And once that happens, once the heart is broken and you recognize it as such, then various paths open to individuals. And there are very many different paths. That's why we should never take a position from one path or another on the other paths, because the broken heart illuminates a path and it is a different path for each broken heart. I understand that when you say the words "broken heart", lots of people just turn off. But the truth is, this is the beginning of wisdom, to understand that you are deeply uncomfortable here. That discomfort illuminates its own solution and it is often years before you take that solution. So you poke around at the different solutions that are available. Maybe you come to the ones that are most familiarly articulated, your own religion. Most of the religions around are pretty good for that. It may be a political solution. It may be an ascetic solution. It may be a hedonistic solution. None of us has the right to judge other people's solutions to suffering. I went to that Zen master's retreat and stayed the better part of a month. It was too rigorous for me. The master was Japanese and the abbot was German and I would find myself walking around in the snow wearing sandals at night as part of the walking meditation and thought this was the revenge of the Second World War. They got all these idealistic American kids and were torturing them. I went over the wall, but a couple of things lingered with me and I went back. It is a deep sense of doubt that drives you into the meditation hall, and often it is a self you discover and cannot stand, which is why you drop it.'*

That is also what Leonard Cohen did initially. But self-deceit was not for him. Self-torture, self-castigation was what he needed for his self-examination, and so he returned to the mountain, not as a follower, but as a searcher. Repeatedly he expressed this as follows: *'I met this old man and I liked what he was not saying.'* His second stay confirmed to Cohen the mental freedom, the importance of the Buddhist exercises and the spirituality of the monastery. This would make him return regularly from 1970 in a continuous process of reorientation and reinstating his self-discipline. The Eastern interpretation of thinking, considered to be the sixth human sense, which concentrates on the consciousness of each individual, became ever more important to him. His original faith, Judaism, was more a way of life than a belief system. In Zen, Cohen discovered a way of life specifically geared to the negation of any system or a binding confession of faith. That freedom fascinated him enormously.

With *Recent Songs* the artist rounded off his first Zen period. Cohen was alone again. His mother had passed away; wife and children had virtually disappeared from his life. The tie to Roshi only got stronger, his interest in Zen deeper. The album and the tour that followed proved to be both an end and a new beginning. Leonard Cohen was thinking and working differently, the culmination of which would follow in the *Book of Mercy* and in *Various Positions*. Asked about his religious aspirations at the launching of the  and record the bard replied that he had no ambition whatsoever to lead a religious life or a life full of prayer. Cohen: *'It is not my nature. I am out on the street, hustling with all the others. What the real high calling behind any life is, is very difficult for me to determine. It goes all the way from thinking that nothing any of us do is terribly important to feeling that every person has a divine spark and is here to fulfil a special mission.'*

While the new perceptions of the artist had consequences, at first only for the content of his work, the qualitative consequences pushed him so high a few years later that for the first and only time in his life, Leonard Cohen warranted the predicate superstar. In some countries, he sold more CDs than the pop idols of the day and icons of the hit parade. To him this was a very ambiguous experience. Nobody is insensitive to success. At the same time, the ironic connoisseur remained unmoved before all toadying. Eventually, when the dust settled, the big silence set in. Liberated from most material day-to-day worries, the grey celebrity did not want more fame, more possessions or more money. Rather, he opted for a definitive entry in the monastery. Cohen chose to spend his days with the wise old man that Roshi is, accepting what every new day would bring them. The final note of a deep friendship between a son who never had the opportunity to hate his father and a grandfather who never faced the hardship of having children he could love. Leonard Cohen and Sasaki Roshi, twenty-first successor in the Zen Buddhist patriarchy, first in line when there is something to drink. Leonard Cohen: *'As I say, the ideas in Zen, I'm not sure what they are because I have only known one old man and I do not know how authentically he represents his tradition. I just know that he has provided a space for me to do the kind of dance with the Lord that I could not find in other places. Something passionate and non-negotiable.'*

The connection to Roshi's *rinzai*, generally considered the most rigorous form of Zen, perfectly suits a man with Cohen's feel for discipline. At the same time, it weighs on him. Though Zen, according to the widest interpretation, may well offer a spiritual foundation for humanity in our present global society and a refuge to many, Leonard Cohen is the last to propagate the faith. In his eyes, Zen is dangerous. Certainly for people who expected salvation from it. *'The romantic idea is that of a tranquil, silent, perfect monastery for a solitary life, but the reality is the exact opposite. There are no private spaces; you are always with people. Zen is a practice which is involved in a very rigorous lifestyle, which – having a kind of fascist militaristic nature – I find very appropriate to the style of life that I want to live. I find if I do not commit myself to that kind of schedule, I will just lose myself in a pool of self-indulgence. So it is a kind of hospital that I live in; it is the land of broken hearts, where people do not know how to do the most basic activities. They do not know how to breathe, they do not know how to walk, they do not know how to sit, they do not know how to shit, they do not know how to do anything. I am one of those people. And so I gratefully embrace this regime, because it is so inhuman that it brings out your humanity. It enables me to locate some small reservoir of self-respect.'*

Daily reality on Mount Baldy is indeed a meagre experience. Two-thirty at night Cohen gets up. The bell that will wake everybody resounds at three, but the ex-artist needs the extra minutes and the accompanying coffee to find himself and possibly write down a few things. After tea in the *zendo*, the meditation space, it is off to the hall where the twenty-four pages of the *Heart Sutra* are to be sung. Not a meditative text, rather a collection of sounds, the *Heart Sutra* stimulates the intestines to vibrate and create a feeling of wellbeing. Afterwards, the group moves into the meditation space for a few hours. The master gives every apprentice a question to which a 5-minute reply has to be given. The technique, the spiritual procedure to mold that answer so that it constitutes a closed whole, is more important than the actual content of question and answer. Then breakfast waits, there are domestic chores, and everyone gets 20 minutes to himself, just enough to brush your teeth and make your bed. Next come a few hours of maintenance: cooking, raking, carpentry, plumbing or paintwork. Because the colony sits about 6000 feet (2000 meters) above sea level, there is quite a lot of snow that needs to be shoveled, for months. The inhabitants share all that is necessary to keep the old scout camp going. At noon everyone again puts on the habit for lunch and a half-hour of rest, following which all continue to work until dinner. After the meal there is a final meditation session lasting two to three hours. Every four weeks there is a *sesshin*, a meeting of heart and mind that amounts to an intensive period in which one sits quietly in the *zendo*. After three to four months the training period is over. Everyone is awakened an hour later and the rhythm of life becomes less strictly delineated. Until the next training period.

The weekly routine is regularly interrupted with a daily, three-hour meeting in the *roshi*, which is the space of the master. These meetings are all about discipline, and include physical beatings. They can cause confusion, depression and – strangely enough – summon a somewhat hollow state that may lead to new directions of thought or total lack of substance. Cohen: *'There is a bias against religious virtue here, and it is very appealing. You never have the feeling that it is Sunday school. You never have the feeling that you are abandoning some cavalier life, or getting into some goody-goody enterprise. Not at all. Not at all.'*

Cohen's passion for routine is evident when you hear him explain convincingly and in detail how things work in the monastery. The essence to him, however, is the content. Even the official certificate from the county of San Bernardino that deems him – as the member of a monastic order – qualified *'to work as a waiter, busboy, or cook'* cannot change that. Cohen finds the meditations, alternated with the hard labor and combined with the chronic lack of sleep, very instructive. As a person you get so tired that you lack the desire to think much about yourself. You are using so much energy that you have to find a balance for yourself to keep up with the system, regardless of how you feel. During *za-zen*, the hours of aimless sitting, you then suddenly have time. Seas of time. Asked about the essence of Zen, the answer of the patriarch is always: *'Vast emptiness and nothing special'*. There is no doctrine, no conviction filled with passion. Even a compulsory catechism and the interpretations thereof are lacking. Only endless space awaits you to think out mental constructions. The worship does not consist of the following of rules. It comes from you. Buddhism does not apply itself to intellectual exercises in thought or moral issues. The only commandments of principle are not to murder or steal, not to cause harm, and not to lie. And even those are just general directives. It is all about soul-searching: who or what you are, will be. The fundamental, underlying point of departure is that people use rules because a strong negation of their singularity troubles their perception of the world. It is more important to get rid of that than to try and reach a sort of pre-packaged moral purity and codify it in rules and taboos. Buddhism may well embrace morality, but it is far from being a moralistic teaching.

*Zazen* offers Leonard Cohen the ultimate confrontation with his cerebral self. In his words: *'You sit for about eighteen hours a day. You begin to examine the panic of your mind. If you can stay still for any amount of time, anything more than a minute or two, which we rarely ever do, some things are disclosed to you. Of course, you shake your legs after meals and go to the bathroom, that sort of thing, but basically there's nothing but stillness for eighteen hours a day. And everything comes up. All the versions of yourself arise if you sit long enough. Finally, it is the freedom from questions like "What is life?" or "Why are we here?" This is the study of the self – your relationship to this entity that we call the self. One of the things that appealed to me about this particular discipline is that it does not demand an answer. And, free from answer and from question, you experience peace. And peace is the embrace of the absolute.'* Jokingly he adds: *'Of course, you cannot stay in that state too long, because you have to eat and you have to go to the washroom.'* With this, Cohen sounds like an echo of Roshi, who continuously points out the danger of self-satisfaction and contentment with monastic life. It has to be the goal to prepare those present for the world outside. Roshi: *'God's world is good, but you cannot stay there too long – no washrooms there!'*

Many a critical outsider initially considered Cohen's decision to enter into the monastery as a stunt. When it turned out to be definitive, the *communis opinio* is that it was an escape, something Cohen denied vehemently. 'This is the very contrary of dropping out. Most people cannot wait to get home to their house or apartment and shut that door and turn on the TV. To me, that is dropping out. There is a saying: "Like pebbles in a bag, the monks polish each other." You are continually involved with people here in a way you are never involved on the outside. You wake up with it and you go to sleep with it. There is this community. Any tendency toward dropping out is immediately spotted in a community like this.'

Which does not mean that Cohen threw his worldly inclinations totally overboard. Even while officially ordained a Zen Buddhist monk, he rolled off his mountain at certain times and got into bed to watch non-stop TV for a few days. Jikan – the inwardly silent – was then pushed aside. And Leonard Cohen reemerged. All the way, Cohen continued to write. He did so with unflagging zeal, inside and out of the monastery. Letting go of his writing to fully give himself to meditation? Out of the question. Cohen: 'That would be the approach of a monk, but I am not a monk. I can very easily call someone and go out for dinner in LA, if I feel like it. The truth is that I enjoy this lifestyle and I enjoy the old guy's company. He is my drinking buddy, you know. Roshi and I have been drinking together for twenty years.'

The first palpable result of his years as writer/monk on and around Mount Baldy comes with the intense and deliberate observations that support Ten New Songs. Moving and full of consolation as an old, lost friend who has returned against all logic, Cohen tells, in a grumbling voice that sounds as if comes directly out of the womb, that he wants to let go. 'I don't trust my inner feelings; inner feelings come and go,' we hear. After years of fighting with the monster within he has finally succeeded in ignoring himself.

When, without any obvious reason, the veil of depression lifted, Cohen's life became not easier, but simpler. Cohen: 'The backdrop of self-analysis I had lived with disappeared. It happened to me by imperceptible degrees and I could not really believe it. I could not really claim it for some time. I thought

51

*there must be something wrong. It is like taking a drink of cold water when you are thirsty. Every taste bud on your tongue, every molecule in your body says thank you.'*

Custom reconciles us to everything. Edmund Burke knew it; now Leonard Cohen lived the experience. Combined with the knowledge that he had no talent whatsoever to lead a spiritual but limited life, it placed him back in the forest of people, where he took up his task. The deep connection with Roshi and the monastic community remained, but Cohen's focus would once again be on what has always been the basis of his existence: his role as an authentic minstrel.

Chapter 7

ASHES OF EXPERIENCE

One could postulate that every religion is the creation of man and thus says nothing about the truth. Going further, you know that the one truth does not exist, at least not so that we can comprehend it. Life then should be about sincerity. Truthfulness in what our heart tells us to strive for, and in what we choose to be. Anything less than this is a weak bid, to be written on the debit side in the balance sheet of our spirit, that purveyor of words and deeds, in charge of and responsible for how we stand in the world.

This vision is purest during adolescence. The big fabrications are over. At the threshold of adulthood, a pregnant will drowns out everybody and everything. Dilettantism and professionalism are involved in a rearguard action.

The winner will be the one who makes our wishes come true or approximates them the closest. When talking about the years of his adolescence. Leonard Cohen remarks that his main sensation was a continuous longing. A comment that seconds the observation made in *The Favorite Game* that deprivation is the mother of all poetry. Being isolated induces dreams. Every person looks for some sort of compensation for his or her shortcomings. Combined with a linguistically strong education, this longing will soon manifest itself. A starting base that's aimed at self-determination and drawing on one's own forces and possibilities will be equally influential.

When hardly sixteen, seventeen years old, I was the editor and publisher of a commercially available magazine. At the same age Cohen wrote his first poems. Of course, we later forget how and who we were at that age. We forget that something like fifteen-year-old wisdom exists, that it has its value just as much as every age's wisdom. As long as we stay true to our points of departure, that does not need to be a fundamental problem. Unfortunately, many of us plunge into puerile flight routes as soon as the great longing seems to be veering off course. Not so the protagonists of this book. However young, vulnerable and even fragile, life and the road we chose demanded an unconditional loyalty to our choices, averse to every 'but' or 'maybe'.

Notwithstanding his seeming non-conformism, not taking on the priesthood and his refusal to take up a place in the family business, Cohen in his own way would fulfil an important role. In Hebrew literature, the writer who is willing to defend his own people or go against them is imputed with a sheer Messianic dimension. Hand in hand with the development of his poetry, the young poet learned to play the piano, and, with the emergence of rhythm and blues, also the guitar, the instrument of the new music. Side by side, poetry and popular music grew up with him, a situation that is further reinforced with the introduction of LPs in 1948.

Just like my partner in crime a few decades earlier, I have built up a record collection since my childhood. Eclectic and honest, these records had a lasting influence. The music molded me, alienated me from the barely elevating life in my provincial town. Content, I looked out at diversity in the world, the contrasts, the (im)possibilities. Wonderful! Without effort, nurturing my creativity became more important than finding employment or striving for financial security by alternative means. Casually, I sacrificed comfort to dreams, determined to make them come true, one by one if necessary. Brel knew it: *'Quand on essaie quelque chose, on n'est jamais malheureux!'* *(If one tries something, one is never unhappy!)* At first I still hid behind the achievements of others that I helped bring into the market and coached. However, after a few years my modesty yielded enough to make room for a paper-thin layer of self-confidence. The start of Book 1.

Cohen's *Book 1,* although still markedly conservative in its wording, contains a selection of poetry showing clearly the two tendencies the artist combines. Readers find clearly delineated positive or negative poems, strengthened in their existence thanks to a mixture of religion and sensuality peculiar to the era from which they were created. I, for my first appearance, showed off with a heavyweight musical biography. Today I am astonished at that. I couldn't go that far any more. So much effort, so much sacrifice. Each in his own way, a debutant invariably seems to search for a creation that passes his own, logical limits.

> *Artes odit nemo nisi ignarus*
> *(Only an ignoramus does not care for art)*
> Unknown

Artistic talent brings you into conflict with yourself. Unavoidably. Life might well be the only valuable possession of a human being, but how you live it determines how you stand in the world as an individual, and the feeling it gives you. If you choose words as your tool, you hardly start out from an enviable position. You are up against a true ocean of books and poetry, an avalanche of characters. The universe would appear far more interesting if, over the ages, mankind had perfected the high art of crossing out irrelevance. Of course, the naked fact remains that people exist by the grace of stories. And each story told is an interpretation. That is why stories reappear, why we constantly create new ones, and why we like to tell them with so many layers so that plenty of interpretations are possible. You can love the writing and the storytelling because it is totally yours to shape. Just the same, you can be the sort of author who simply cannot get away from it. Dixit Cohen: *'A scheme is not a vision.'* There lies the difference between writers who 'do their thing' and the others, who work with their whole being.

*'I came so far for beauty, I left so much behind.'* It appears to subscribe perfectly to what part of the artistic world so eagerly promotes: the artist seen as asocial, in opposition to the dominant culture, always at the defense of change and renewal.

That vision, however, is rather artificial, although creative people are indeed truly individualistic. And that is a good thing. Oscar Wilde already argued in his time that individualism is a disruptive and destabilizing power of immense value. He who is serious about what he wants to generate has no other choice than to render the most individual expression of the most individual experience in his work. Of course, this creates inner doubt. A sheer unalienable loneliness is your part. At the same time, you realize that you do have a voice which needs to be heard. Life has not dealt you a non-speaking part. In the evolution of many traditional writers, searching for the relationship between their singularity and the world follows their discovery of self, to evolve later in life into a laconic mild compassion. This stands in stark contrast to the above. A person like Cohen does not walk the line of that romanticized image. He is a messenger, without splendid or prettified details, almost lapidary in a way. Staying in touch with what is essential, that is what it is all about, and walking the road towards it with a lot of empathy. Doing so, he refuses to fall back on a specific point of view or a unified writing style that traditionally pulls together the oeuvre of a writer. A person sings because he is happy or, as it happens, very unhappy. To forget something, or to remember. An author writing from sensory perception writes for exactly the same reasons. His stories have to come out, each with their own individuality. To blaze a trail for themselves in the world, to witness.

Many writers argue that writing leads to not living. That is wrong. Maybe you stand outside of everyday life, but not outside of life itself. You distil it. A writer turns inward, lives reclusively. In contrast to the fallow land that would be a setback to many, he or she finds there a source of life. A place full of luxuriant sobriety, to describe it with a typical Cohen concept. Colleague-author Irving Layton sees in each serious writer a person chockfull of conflicts, who knows how to reconcile his internal struggle in his work. *'That place is the harbor. It does not set the world in order. It does not really change anything. It just is a kind of harbor; it is the place of reconciliation, it is the consolamentum, the kiss of peace.'*

Layton makes it sound restful. But this reality only arrives at the end of the process, when you can look back with painful affection. Before you get to that point, you have to fight yourself with sheer melancholic masochism. Settle the accounts! In the first instance with the intentions you might have as an author. Does the reader understand that one hint? The underlying idea? Your fundamental range of ideas? The ultimate goal? Questions like whiplashes to the mind of the author pouring his eyes out in front of the computer screen wanting to know who followed him up to this place. And, dear reader, was it worth your while? However, tempting, forget these questions! It does not matter what an author puts in his text, what his interpretation, evaluation or take on it is. If his point of departure was honest, he has given what he had and has not delivered a fleeting description. If it is honest, he might touch a person in his humanity. As Max Frisch remarked years ago: *'You are what you are. You hold the pen as if it were a needle in a seismological institute. In fact, it is not we who are writing, we are being written. Writing means: reading yourself.'*

Even more sensitive than the struggle with his intentions is the confrontation of the author with his métier. Readers have to be captivated. The religious vocabulary, so suited to transmit emotions, forms an unmistakable and often subconscious part of our Western pattern of thinking and thus can help. Cohen's work makes this abundantly clear. Modern icons have an almost equal impact, certainly when their life story is imbedded in a religious ground note. Yet for both of us, starting invariably from our cultural frame of reference, neither is ever more than a support. You can create a passive main character to make the inward voyage of discovery or use an existing person to clarify your vision, but whatever option you choose, your personality's limitations regularly weigh you down, constrict you. Cohen: *'I have had this urgency from quite young, quite a young age, to make things, you know. Mostly it was on a page. Just to make something that worked. Something that rose off the page, that sang, that had a life of its own. That could win a heart. Could present me in a good light, could touch myself. I always experience myself as falling apart, and I am taking emergency measures. I try Prozac. I try love. I try drugs. I try Zen meditation. I try the monastery. I try forgetting about all those strategies and going straight. And the place where the evaluation happens is where I write the songs, when I get to that place where I cannot be dishonest about what I've been doing. It begins with an appetite to discover my self-respect. To redeem the day. So the day does not go down in debt. It begins with that kind of appetite.'*

Cohen regularly uses the image of a man on his knees. That humble position to him is the basis of the later end result, regardless of whether it is reached with regular language or with an enlarged interpretation of reality. Leonard Cohen: *'I have never written with the luxury of choice. My songs have come to me. I have had to scrape them out of my heart. They came in pieces, at a time, in showers and fragments...I cannot dispose the song to any situation or anything in the political realm. It has always been torn from myself. If it has any value, it is because it has been created in a certain kind of furnace that gives it a certain kind of quality, and it is nothing I can determine. I do not have to win a vote; I do not have to establish a system that does not contradict itself; I do not have to have a clear vision. I do not even have to have a vision. All I have to do is report things as accurately as I can from moment to moment.'*

In contrast to myself, the Canadian seldom steps back from his own life. Cohen catches his human folly in a butterfly net and pins it down against an all-dominating background of faith with an undertone of humor that puts things in perspective. His work is not that of a man baring his soul, but of a searcher. He explores his soul and allows us to witness the inner landscape that he discovers during his search. Important in this is to divest himself of all ballast, all superfluous stories, all versions of him that do not matter until all that is left are the bare essentials. This remainder he has to defend, if only because he does not have anything else left. Leonard Cohen: *'I have to go beneath my opinions, which long ago I ceased to have any great interest in. My own opinions are predictable. I can dredge them up in a conversation over a drink to keep the talk flowing. And I feel the same way about beliefs: my beliefs are predictable, and I find them kind of tiresome. So I need to write a lot to avoid the opinion, the belief or the slogan, and to come up with the freshness that determines the living quality of a piece of work. You shatter versions of the self, until you get down to a line, a word, that you can defend, that you can wrap your voice around without choking.'*

Writing as an artistic process without compromise. A somewhat old-fashioned image. Unattainable in the eyes of many. And yet, although a writer today has to deliver himself into the hands of commerce and does not get a chance to show what he has when he does not play that game, it is still possible to work in a traditional artistic way under a relative lee, with time on your side. A lonely and honest choice towards yourself and your public. Hermetically enclosed in your world you live with the obligation to rediscover, reinvent yourself. You grasp an idea in full flight, try to hold on to it and put it on paper in a sensible way. Like an obsessive fanatic you slave away, surrendering to what drives you. Your passion is all fire, burns you up, destroys what it offered in the first place. Your commitment exceeds the limits of the acceptable and permissible. The guest becomes a tyrant, takes over and no longer allows you to peacefully find your way. Besmirches paper. You have to fight back. Stand up straight and with dignity in the eye of the storm. Extremely difficult and exhausting, as the world is not at all geared to let people keep and profess their singularity. But your commitment is complete. What in the end survives on paper is the most purified, the ashes of your experience. Exhausted you pull yourself up. Your blood still tingling in your fingers you stagger away from your desk.

In other words, reality brings the so-called placid writers' existence. But even though there is no sign of luxury, you cannot hazard to speak of a real choice either. It is so. This is what you do, without further merit. Leonard Cohen: *'It is something you do every day and you cannot get too far from it, otherwise you forget what it is about. I am speaking of degree. I always thought that I sweated over the stuff. But I had no idea what sweating over the stuff meant until I found myself in my underwear crawling along the carpet in a shabby room at the Royalton Hotel unable to nail a verse. Knowing that I had a recording session and knowing that I could get by with what I had but that I am not going to be able to do it. When I tried to sing it, I realized it came from my boredom and not from my attention. It came from my desire to finish the song and not from the urgency to locate a construction that would engross me. It is just a matter of intensity. I was still able to juggle stuff: a life, a woman, a dream, other ambitions, other tangents. At a certain point I realized I only had one ball in my hand, and that was The Song. Everything else had been wrecked or compromised and I could not go back, and I was a one-ball juggler. I would do incredible things with that ball to justify the absurdity of the presentation.'*

Producing work that has a will of its own, work showing stature and courage is what it is all about. Coquettish linguistic frills, hollow rhetoric, excessive multiplicity and lifeless intellectualism are the obstacles. The author, that strange soul that we are, chooses directness over purple prose. Sensitive, intimate descriptions give so much more depth than a text that is chasing itself without let-up. At the same time there is doubt. Brel, who could characterize the Flemish like no other, told a journalist how that bizarre half of Belgium never would think of saying *'I love you like I love this flower.'* No, that is not enough. *'I love you like this mountain,'* they will say, proceeding to describe the whole mountain painstakingly. Terrible. The consequence being that he who chooses for less, for sensitivity, for a text in which the words and the silences in between define the experience, goes against the dominant nature. Modesty and subdued silence, language in which one can die, continuously loses out against the proliferation of symbolism and a language literally bursting at the seams.

On you go. Looking for the ultimate book. For the song turning the tide. That one fragment of text that stops your breath. The alchemy that allows you to refine ugliness into beauty. Your unique self, more alive on paper than in reality. What the author wants to see in print is nothing less than that 'I' who understands you, in your complexity and simplicity, better than you yourself will ever do.

> *I know it must have hurt you,*
> *it must have hurt your pride*
> *to stand beneath my window*
> *with your bugle and your drum,*
> *while I was waiting*
> *for the miracle*
> *for the miracle to come*
> Leonard Cohen

*Beautiful Losers*, Cohen's tour de force, left the obscure poet-writer who enjoyed cult status in small groups, empty. *The New York Times* proclaimed it *'one of the works of the decade'*, but it did not sell at all. The famous and revered free sixties were not free enough for this combination of eroticism and violence. The distorted biblical scenes, the longing to let go of cohesion and the fear to be able to do so. All of it together made *Beautiful Losers* frightening and repulsive. The author had expected to pay his bills with the proceeds from the book. Instead he got stuck. He was a writer who did not sell. One that urgently needed a financial aid. Cohen decided to travel to Nashville. Music City, USA, the capital of country. Maybe his poems could work as country songs. When his plane touched down in New York, he wound up checking into the Chelsea Hotel. The Chelsea. People, diverse as Dylan Thomas and Sid Vicious, stayed there, along with a few hundred other writers, musicians and artists. Cohen: *'Once I hit the Chelsea Hotel, there was no turning back.'* The Canadian was well received in the artistic community. Judy Collins accepted some of his songs, and soon his signature was on a record deal.

Whereas Dylan had already opened a door using texts that until then had been unusual in pop music, Cohen's role seemed to explore the world behind that door. The mix of his poetic sensitivity, the surroundings in Montreal where he had grown up, and the influence of the Beat writers led to unprecedented results. As the only one, he succeeded in placing classical poetry in an acceptable rock context, with the possible exception of one or two good songs by Lou Reed, another destroyed soul. The word, forever his bane, would be disseminated in that way from this point forward.

While it seems logical that success would have pleased Cohen, instead he felt an uncomfortable prisoner of opposites. The literary world that spit him out because he chose pop music for the money, and the rock critics who did not understand him were intimidated by his work and failed to come up with anything more serious than the cliché of the tormented neurotic who builds a career on his morbidity, when describing his work. Cohen: *'Confusing seriousness with gloominess is wrong. We can be destroyed just as easily by mindless frivolity as we can by obsessive depression.'*

Cohen's critics turned out to be unable to see beyond their own noses. Not the framework – the song, the book – defines the quality, but the content and its impact. The non-recognition of those designated for such tasks may be troublesome; all the same it brings a kind of tranquility, something affirmative. In the end, almost all work that has true appeal is somewhat subversive, a very desirable trait.

Meanwhile, year after year, time carves new paths. With or against the wind, the miller grinds. The contemporary image of the author is no longer the loner living near the outer fringe, the writer whose texts are deeply infused with correctness and sensitivity. More and more, the image portrayed has become that of a brutal rake on TV. Against this background Cohen and a small group of kindred spirits demonstrate that you do not necessarily have to stoop down to clownery if you want to trace your own route in this world and find a livable position. It is perfectly possible to keep your 'I' pure and not howl with the wolves in the forest. You can be a beautiful loser!

Chapter 8

L'OR DU TEMPS

*Well, you know that I love to live with you*
*But you make me forget so very much*
*I forget to pray for the angels*
*And then the angels forget to pray for us*
Leonard Cohen

A thousand years ago, when Leonard Cohen wrote the above words, his struggle was not yet over. The memories of a room that would follow, his *Songs From a Room*, evoked the one who was no longer there. In sparsely decorated rooms where *'there is only one prayer'* he waited the whole night *'for your step on the stairs'*, underscoring the saying that it is good to hope, but bad to count on your hope.

The impossibility of his relationship with Marianne Ihlen had already been incorporated in his poems in *Flowers for Hitler*. At that time still with hope: *Slowly I Married Her*. In *Parasites of Heaven* Cohen already knew better. In that poem he spoke about his *'uncaptured darling'* and the many nightmares he just could not escape. He rounded off with the painfully forced conclusion *I Guess It's Time To Say Goodbye*. He, a Cohen, predestined by the tradition he is part of. She, not only a divorcée with a child, but what is more, a female goyim, a non-Jewess. To many it may be incomprehensible that a relationship would disintegrate for these reasons. At best one can try to surmise what it means to be born and raised within Cohen's tradition. How heavy law and tradition weigh. No judgment can be expected to ignore the reality and riches of that image.

For the Chassidim, the spirit is not more important than the body, nor the other way around. A man and a woman who come together is a feast, a synthesis of yin and yang, of the human

64

and the godly. A feast that may and even has to be celebrated frequently. Sexuality and philosophy are complementary expressions of *le phénomène humain* (the human condition). In the Talmud it is written at the end of the *kiddushin*: *'When a man is standing in front of his Maker, he will have to account for those (God given) pleasures he did not use.'* Leonard Cohen: *'The idea that there is a staircase of gold and marble which leads to knowledge is seductive, but it seems to me that the idea of some-thing needing to get broken before we can learn anything is a more true idea*.' It is my experience. Maybe you can escape it, but I doubt it. Unless the heart breaks, we will never know anything about love. As long as our objective universe does not collapse, we will never know anything about the world. We think that we know the mechanism, but only when it fails do we understand how intricate and mysterious is the operation. So, it is true, *'there is a crack in everything'*... all human activity is imperfect and unfinished. Only that way can we have the notion that there is something inside us that can only be located through disillusion, bad luck and defeat. Unfortunately, that seems to be the case.'

The self-declared *tourist of beauty* sounds fairly resigned, but he certainly does not keep at bay the dynamics of relationships. Raw, destructive emotions populate his poems and songs. Obsessions alternate with light-heartedness, distance with unity, and grim lack of illusion with undiluted melancholy. From *Beautiful Losers* the conclusion can be drawn that we find ourselves in a world filled with obscene and brutal emotionality. Delving in these emotions, desperately reaching there for a touch of grace, is an act of almost absolute love. The union of body and spirit is central. *'For a blessed second truly I was not alone.'*

The theme would continue to come up in his work. Notwithstanding all their striving for artistry and authenticity, women simply are the best that can happen to men in their unfilled existence. At that moment in life, women are indispensable for Cohen to reconcile him with himself and with

65

the world. What the critic of *Sounds* described at the time as *'possibly the most beautiful album someone can own'* did not miss its entrance in the Hendrickx home. This lump of human need, despair and loneliness filled dreams in a new room. *'It seems so long ago, Nancy was alone.'* We are all scandalously emotional, however we portray ourselves in public. Nancy, a redhead beauty with the naturalness of a wild forest nymph was to me as unattainable as the inaccessible Aryan Ice Queen Nico had been for Cohen. She got the record. I got the memory. A new love seemed the softest possible flight. An opportunity for taking distance from mere sensuality and to actually project the mother role in my life. Without being blind to what a wiser man described as *'the thistle in the kiss'* the choice for this tender engagement was conscious and permanent.

Regardless to whatever degree ideological differences, faith and convictions recede for amorousness and sexuality, sooner or later love finds its own rhythm and course. Arrived at that point the path once again lies wide open for the other focal points in the life of a human being. The ruins then are under full construction. Of course, nobody distances him or herself of a longing until it is thoroughly lived. No woman lets her love and commitment in a relationship die as long as she hopes that she can bend the course of affairs to her will. As long as she sees compensations for everything she feels is lacking in her relationship.

Men are much less intensely implicated in the daily experience and filling out of their life. They accept off-hand that their relations will endure, just as long as things are fairly good, without delving too deep into the exact content or the concept of 'love'. Seldom or never do men see the collateral damage an intimate bond sustains throughout the years.

And as the wind tears the leaves off a tree, so time will take their loved one away from them. The absolute end comes to them almost without fail as a thunderbolt in a clear sky. An unforeseeable calamity, against which the emotionally chanceless man will fight with all his might and against better knowledge, if necessary, with a plea literally torn from his heart and drenched in tears.

*Warm spotted butterfly*
*Words are meagre, breakable and brittle.*

*How can they, powerless victims of my turbulent mind, ever do justice to you, your persona and the un-nameable impact you have upon my life?*

*You, who delighted my life at a moment when disconsolateness held me tight in its grip. Fresh, inwardly untouched, you gave yourself up to a melancholic, who discovered in you the strongest medicine. A man marked by repudiation found healing, slaked himself at your source, and returned to the living.*

*Afterwards, time and the cynicism of this world regularly took possession of us, but never, never did we get caught for good. Your enthusiasm, my enthusiasm, propelled our love out of the valley of shadows, till far above the clouds, from where we looked down smiling on the teeming mass beneath.*

*Like a butterfly is your mind. Care-free fluttering, sure of a positive course, enjoying a beautiful melody, a pleasant conversation or enriching movie, or concentrated and contained coming down to a space where depth and content are under discussion, carefully filling itself with all available information, weighing and measuring, deciding what course will be followed. Beautiful is your mind. Dependable in its honesty, openness and self-assuredness, overwhelming by its ability not to judge, but on the contrary leaving space to each idea, each vision and version, prepared to compare the respective truths with each other or after careful consideration condense them, each in its own value.*

*Rich is your mind. By the breath of the spectra you encompass, the understanding you try to bring, the gentleness with which you judge and the strong and firm impression you leave with anybody lucky enough to be allowed to know you better than a superficial meeting would grant. To me, the luckiest of all, your advise is priceless, your support the ground on which I walk and attaining your approval, appreciation or admiration is the highest, the most impressive reward.*

*Like a butterfly is your body. Tinted with colorful specks, giving a unique pigment to each part. Down the striking coal, outpost in your always provoking, blindingly beautiful neck I* descend, caressing your warm skin, down to your naughty curly hair. There, as if hidden in the coppice, hides a second eye of the butterfly, with a wink welcoming, inviting me, the considerate visitor.

A birthmark cannot be missing from this mischievous spectacle, revealing itself on a softly undulating fold, along which I trace a way back upwards. Here, as an angel with his folded wings, the butterfly shows it richest camouflage in a variegated spectacle, leading as an apotheosis to a highly seductive pigmentation of your ear-lobe.

Beautiful is your body. By its radiance, purity and the naturalness it emanates, unselfconsciously inviting endearments, which it accepts complacently without affectation or ceremony, but sincerely and consciously loyal. Beauty and power in a near perfect combination, affecting a man so much more than the artificiality of top models and 'perfect' sizes.

Rich is your body. From your voluptuous bosom, which you dare to flaunt suggestively with righteous pride, over your glorious, man friendly nipples to the melting warm inside of your thighs, you offer me nothing less than paradise on earth. And then I hardly dare expand on your godly triangle, synonym to me of the word passion in its most emphatic expression. To be allowed to caress your buttocks, be able to feel the glowing pores of your back under my hands, they are physically the most penetrating, most lasting moments in a man's life.

I, who try to color your life, to fill you with joy and happiness, want to go on doing this, staking all I can give you. You always coveted the life in me. Going on, rough and ready, stubbornly, with the tide or diametrically opposed to it. In that feeling we were and are connected as no two others can be. It is enriching to think that in the future even more than in the past we will cherish this kind of unity, if both of us make the deliberate choice to do so.

Words are meagre, breakable and brittle.

How can they, powerless victims of my turbulent mind, ever do justice to us, our relationship and its un-nameable impact on our life?

Marc Hendrickx

Then it is over, for good. With a stomach full of emptiness you register the complaint. Words, hurting like blows of a fist. The building blocks of a writer. Not in the least did you ever expect this material to be used so destructively against you. By her! No critic or reviewer, however vindictive or negative, has such powerful weapons at his disposal.

> *You let me love you till I was a failure –*
> *There are many ways a man can serve his time*
> Leonard Cohen

Whether you are dumped pontifically or inconsequentially, it is always love with a raw edge. Through the phenomenon of memory, you notice that time does not really exist. In the beginning there is lust, spurred on by your drives, the escape from time. Then you are all in love with someone she might have been. Later you look back. Nostalgia for lost loves resembles the undefined longing for the games you played as a child. Everything is different; returning impossible. You live in a different now.

Leaving Marianne, contrary to what many assumed, Leonard Cohen never had a relationship with the woman who served him *'tea and oranges'*. Suzanne Vaillancourt, a ravishing beauty and the wife of a friend who was a painter, let the opportunity for fleeting intimacy pass. Because the realization of a longing at the same time implies its bankruptcy?

Fact is that the artist, who was fast growing in stature, at the threshold of his first visit to Roshi's cloister was on the verge of falling apart. The sentence *'If I have been unkind'* in his Bird on the Wire puts the problem into focus. Kindness, goodness, described by the rabbis as *'the beginning and the end of the law'*, is considered the ultimate virtue in Judaism. Falling short in this, is about the worst thing one can do wrong. Cohen failed doubly. He had failed his Lord and he had failed his chosen female partner.

There is a passage in the book of Ezekiel in which the

Highest voices his admiration for female beauty: *'I have let you grow like the plants in the field, naked and without clothes. You grew up, taller and reached adulthood, the jewel of jewels. Your breast are fully grown and your pubic hair has grown.'* Leonard Cohen gladly offers his vision: *'I do not think a man ever gets over that first sight of the naked woman. That is Eve standing over him. It is the morning and the dew on the skin. And I think that is the major content of every man's imagination. All the sad adventures in pornography and love and song are just steps on the path towards that holy vision.'* It begs the question what we seek to define as 'holy', or for the non-believers among us, the highest good. Sex? Love? Intimacy? Or do we start our list from the first kiss? All are tainted with the risk of rejection, the possibility that it will not work. With the exception of the most elementary needs in our lives – hunger and thirst, living and health – these are the issues that are most important in our relationship to others. Cohen: *'I guess that the source of all suffering is a sense of separation between you and everything else. That separation is always fictitious but that fiction is always very powerful. Loneliness or emptiness is a fearful condition.'*

At Roshi's a new Suzanne crossed his path. This time, Cohen once again will not marry. He builds the temple, fills the shrine, but refuses to fulfil the rite. Thoughtfully Cohen describes marriage, that grave for love, as *'the real monastery of our times, the real spiritual adventure'*. His struggle with the conventions, with the concubinage of love and calculation, turns up from alpha to omega in his poetry collection *Death of a Lady's Man*. A fragment, bitter as never before:

*Love is a fire*
*It burns everyone*
*It disfigures everyone*
*It is the world's excuse for being ugly*
Leonard Cohen

The drawn-out split-up would be one including all the fun stuff people are so crazy about in a divorce. In *Lover, Lover, Lover* the author positions himself, naming his failure as a Cohen, with all Jewish traditions implied in it, the basis of the crack of doom. In *There Is a War* it transpires overly clearly that the mother of his children cannot bear the fact that he wants at all cost to aspire to naked authorship. In the honest *The Price of This Book* Cohen writes openly and clearly that the result leaves him torn in two. He has to strive to keep his love and his work strictly separated, or give up his *'life in art'*, something *'which a terror will not let me do'*.

Seeking shelter in café, *The Little Opera,* I feel battered, gone to the dogs, lost in the big silence, way past tears, I look for a space to get myself out of the cold and warm up the freezing feeling in my insides. *'It's four in the morning…'* In an atmosphere dominated by the nearness of half-drunks, while no longer seeing a way ahead yourself, suddenly there is that song, that voice. Your sad shadow gets company, is no longer the sole one to stand behind you. Time to go. The world is waiting.

From Edgar Allan Poe and Jack Kerouac over the protagonists of this book to the newest generation of youngsters, the vicious circle of an always-new solitude continues to manifest itself. Emotionally stunted you exchange the listlessness of the forever-faithful homely bed for the much praised *buen desco*. Disruptive sexual power. You give prevalence to pleasure over love, fully choosing the Dionysian side of life. *'Though his words were twisted, the naked magic thrived.'* A summons. For women who do not want to be loved, but desired. Yet however unsuspected, the song of praise of eroticism torn from the roaming heart, the quest for physical pleasure, unavoidably lead to confrontations with an emptiness that is quite frankly both crushing and grotesque. Every person who has known sex, with and without love, knows that it is love that makes the physical contact moving and that sex directs love towards the body. It is not because your sensuality runs away with you that you can continue to look upon women solely as sexually interesting creatures.

> *O chosen love, O frozen love*
> *O tangle of matter and ghost*
> *O darling of angels, demons and saints,*
> *And the whole broken-hearted host*
> *Gentle this soul*
> Leonard Cohen

The contra point of Cohen douses the fire in the loins. He himself describes his masterwork *The Window* as an oratorio that allows both parts of the soul to come together. More than that, it is a creation in which he manages to voice the ultimate confluence of God and woman, without explicitly using the words beauty or solace. Even though that is what it is about all the time. Desire is exchanged for peace. The aspiration of a meeting with godliness is, just for an instant, as in a state of grace, made good. *'Then lay your rose on the fire...'*

Nobody leaves the battle unscathed. A strong antidote is more than welcome. Still you keep each new lost love in your fingers. You taste her; try to keep her close that way, even though you wash her away irrevocably. And so even though you feel *'so close to everything that we've lost'*, it is lost. Forever. The plus in it is that you cannot ruin it once more... *'We'll never have to lose it again.'* Leonard Cohen: *'Although people change, and their bodies change and their hair grows grey and falls out and their bodies decay and die, I think that there is something that does not change. About love, and about the feelings we have for people. Marianne... When I hear her voice on the telephone, I know that something is completely intact, even though our lives have separated and we have gone on very different paths. I feel that love never dies and that when there is an emotion strong enough to gather a song about it, that there is something about that emotion that is indestructible.'*

The poet has come a long way since that day at St Lawrence River. He now realizes that you cannot just choose to travel blind if you want to arrive someplace. He does not give up on love, but knows that it will take time and discipline to arrive at it. Moreover, he is aware that it will always take second place to his writing. And so, another relationship turns to nothing. Cohen misses depth, connectedness and togetherness. Total union is impossible to attain when both partners do not share the same spiritual attitude, postulates the romantic. Total unity is impossible to achieve, period. Years full of struggle are not to be this time. The artist is silenced, until he returns from his retreat with *Book of Mercy*, a collection of psalms that allows him to stand in the world once again.

The first year I was fully aware of my marriage to authorship, it turned out to be the proven medicine against sadness, homesickness and melancholy. Without *la fièvre juponnière* there reigned an almost banal restfulness. No shocking tragedy, no emotional empathy, only paper. Later steps brought me in the direction of the theatre, in the direction of this book, ever so slowly. Then, all of a sudden, there was an opening. A difficult, but welcome relationship formed an addition to my life as a slightly nostalgic eccentric. No coincidence. *'When you get out of the way of your own love it becomes true, when it is not fixed, when it is not solidified and when it is not focused rigidly on another object, it broadcasts in front of you and in back of you, to the right of you, to the left of you, above you and beneath you and in the center of a force field that includes everything, that has no inside and no outside, that does not look at anything, nor does it need to be looked at.'*

A ferryman. A man giving soul to life. Many young women think in those kinds of Himalayan concepts. But love exists in so many gradations. Putting across that strong willed 'I will not be denied' is not given to all. If oppression becomes your lot – you too small, the world too big – therefore, flight is the only thing you can think of. To flee. In the arms of your lover if at all possible. Cohen expressed it as follows: *'every heart, every heart to love will come / but like a refugee.'* He too gave it another try. In vain. Cohen: *'I am actively working on songs most of the time. Which is why my personal life has collapsed. Finally, she saw I was a guy who just could not come across in the sense of being a husband and having more children and the rest. I hated it when it was going on, so maybe I would feel better about it now. But I do not think so. What would I be doing? Finding new drugs? Buying more expensive wine? I don't know. This seems to me the most luxurious and sumptuous response to the emptiness of my own existence: religion. Real, profound and voluptuous, delicious entertainment. The real feast that is available to us is within this activity. Nothing touches it.'* A meaningful smile... *'Except if you are courting. If you are young, the hormonal thrust has its own excitement.'*

> *Dared to look up at the light*
> *'been blinded ever since*

Awful amounts of people spend their days in silent despair, without managing to live. They get stuck in a forgotten love and relive the fears and limitations of a past relationship. Time to wake up. Disenchant the fairytale. The two lives that color this book prove that different forms of love, however different, can enrich life. Love, real love, is more than a placebo against existential pain. In the deceivingly seductive *Love Itself*, guitar arpeggio's and subtle piano included, Cohen uses the sunlight as a metaphor for the rays of love in which the Lord applied *'the dust you seldom see'* to define us. In an experience of that order even the need to love dissolves. Ambitions and spiritual aspirations disappear. You can totally, completely relax, let go of yourself, and blend in your ordinary, everyday humanity.

> *I'll try to say a little more:*
> *Love went on and on*
> *Until it reached an open door –*
> *Then Love itself*
> *Love itself was gone*
> Leonard Cohen

Chapter 9

WHEN THE DEVIL GROWS OLD, HE WANTS TO BECOME A MONK

(old Chinese saying)

Through the years Leonard Cohen suggested in his lyrics that the decline and the definitions which disrupt the inner landscape of our mind so thoroughly are in no small way linked to the general state of mind tainting our social structure. He would not be himself if not re-directing the attention to the messenger in doing so: *'What I feel is more or less what other people feel. Not everybody, but a lot of people feel like I do or will feel like I do. I did feel that things were breaking down, but I was breaking down, you know.'*

As slaves to our search, each form of awareness is more a beginning than a goal. Whether a more conscious path leads us through religion, spirituality, culture and relational perfectibility or not, life pushes us on, always and relentless. And we? We follow. We want to lead the dance, sometimes believe, if for a moment, that we are actually doing so. But following while searching and feeling our way is our destiny, that much we have learned in the meantime. Leonard Cohen: *'Human activity is involved with suffering and loss. Anything we do is a triumph over those given realities. Everybody suffers and everybody tries to find a way out of their suffering. Everybody is lonely and everybody tries to find a way out of their loneliness. As you get older, you understand that you must become broken. That the breaking is part of the process of growing up.'*

And so at a riper age you learn to live with your failures. The past no longer glides over your present as if a dark cloud. You know that soon things will be looking up. Soon, you will be freed of all hope. The testament of your pretensions has been written.

To enjoy is not being. Forgetting is the art. Even if life does not seem to be tailored to your size, you no longer suffer from that fact. You stand apart from all competition from then on. Just maybe growing old is a synonym to the acceptance of all loss. In any case, the inner peace linked to reaching a certain age is a coveted commodity. Everybody wants to find peace. Cohen: *'For me it was very much about getting older. I read somewhere that when you approach the end of middle age, the brain cells associated with anxiety start to die, so you are going to start to feel better anyway, whether or not you try to make yourself a holier person. I know a lot of older people who are very worried and bitter, but luckily it has not happened in my case.'* Delving deeper into the matter, the minstrel falls back on his experience in the monastery: *'It was the understanding of not mastering an understanding of what the old master was trying to tell me. I could not break through. I did not really understand it. And maybe I was not meant to understand. Maybe it just had to sink into my heart and make it more relaxing to be alive. But something eased inside me. The only thing that I was completely sure of in my process of becoming a monk was that Roshi understood my difficult and unpleasant inner condition and reacted spontaneously in proportion to it. He ignored or accepted all your small problems and instead he always talked to the fully developed, ripened and enlightened part of your nature. Therefore the things he said were sometimes unintelligible until the understanding was deepened and you realized that he was addressing the most true and intimate part of your heart. From the beginning Roshi addresses the part of you that you want to find, and slowly you become able to see it yourself in an ambiguous, hazy and foggy way.'*

How badly I wanted to write this book, how strong this testimony grew in me! Thirty years younger than Cohen and not enriched by the wise advice of an old Zen master, it required some guts to put together the pillars of this project. After all, one has to face all the facts, no holds barred. The partially unknown as well as the way too familiar and therefore feared facts. Old age and death. Youngsters could not care less. People of a certain age, on the other hand, have an inkling because of the daily sensations and changes they note in themselves. For the Talmud, forty is the age of understanding. The book is wise. At forty you have fewer certainties about your future than ever before, yet you feel better in that situation than one would rationally allow. It is the beginning of a new period. The time to mature. That is the period between forty and sixty: you either grow up or you die. Men grow up late.

> *The older you get, the lonelier you become,*
> *and the deeper the love you need*
> Josua Roshi Sasaki

A situation to be avoided, one in which you rarely meet new people any more, in which hardly anything can still destroy your balance and when virtually nothing is able to fire your enthusiasm. To many these are the images that bear the hallmark of old age. Authors have an unsuspected advantage here: you are almost always alone. Two advantages, given that your contemplative existence is seldom to be destabilized. Heed the warning signal! If your enthusiasm risks being stimulated by cynicism then you are on the wrong track and depression lies in ambush around the corner. Cohen, who in his forties called himself with imperturbable mildness *'too old for suicide'*, looks with sorrow upon the fast growth of suicides amongst depressed old people. Though depression may well be called the sand that polishes the pearl, his battle is over. Leonard Cohen no longer lives as a torn soul who has to fight for a decent existence. And once again he opposes the reigning trend. In spite of the famed quotation by Tennessee Williams – *'Life is a fairly well-written play except for the third act'* – he thoroughly enjoys the process of growing old. It allows him to get a grip on a number of things and to fathom the mysteries of our worldly existence. Perfectly at ease watching the effects of ageing in himself, his friends and his children, an evolution that can easily be considered a rounding-off, Cohen comments favorably: *'It really is the most fascinating activity!'*

Which is not to say that a necessarily slower pace of life and diminishing cockiness rule unabashed. You can still pitch vitality against mortality, the renunciation of expectations. The lyrical young man, the meditative grown-up, the elder looking back, none are irrefutable certainties. Leonard Cohen admits that there might be some truth in the archetypes, but *'the idea that your creative impetus is over by thirty, that you immolate yourself on this pyre of energy and sexuality and can then go back to cleaning up and doing the dishes... it just is not so. The fire continues to burn fiercely as you get older. You can feel even more passionate about things as you get older. As you drop the restraining and inhibiting braces of your thoughts and allow your feelings to become manifest, a certain kind of energy is liberated.'*

Whereas such a burst of energy at a young age might have led to a pushy fierceness, now there is space for a deep carving, almost quietened intimacy. Those who do not wish to seek Eastern wisdom in Cohen's more recent work can easily ascribe its overtly serene character to the wisdom of age, the reflections of a remarkable mind, channeled by time into a new course. Leonard Cohen: *'I think I always cherished some idea of an old man in a suit, smoking a cigarette, and delicately talking about his work to somebody. If you hang in there long enough, you begin to be surrounded by a certain gentleness, and also a certain invisibility. This invisibility is promising, because it will probably become deeper and deeper. And with invisibility – and I am not talking about the opposite of celebrity, I mean something like "The Shadow", who can move from one room to another unobserved – comes a beautiful calm.'*

Reveling in the now: living, writing and enjoying every moment to the fullest. It turns out to be a beautiful combination not to lose your lucidity. Having, same as Cohen, come to understand and found an equilibrium in your isolation, you can grasp far better what it is all about, that trivial, insignificant life of ours. Being able to acquire that wisdom and those insights is of immense value. In the margin of each individual story, without the superfluous memories weighing down one's path of life, you are allowed to live the time you have left without further inner struggle. *'Writing about what made our lives,'* to use the words of Richard Klinkhamer. As a consequence, you, dear reader, can read this book as a preliminary study. As a testament. The balance of a quest for awareness, religion, passion, love. And loss.

> *Lost the budding ways*
> *To escape time*
> *Always November, always rain*
> *Always this heart in vain*
> *Always*
> J.C. Bloem

Chapter 10

SOMETIMES MAN HAS TO MAKE HASTE NOT TO LOSE THE WILL
TO DIE

*The ponies run*
*The girls are young*
*The odds are there to beat*
*You win a while*
*And then it's done*
*Your little winning streak*
Leonard Cohen

Life. Last century one could hardly find a more gullible *bon vivant*/writer than Ernest Hemingway. Fisherman, cat lover, runner of bulls, drunk, womanizer, war correspondent. The list of magnificent descriptions is endless. Yet Hemingway already knew that all stories end in death. Whether you look upon life as a deep grey boat from which you disembark sooner or later, or view your passing as a virtuoso pirouette amidst whirling ashes, it does not really make any difference. You remain a temporary and very relative part. When I was about fourteen years old and had my first revelations in life, I was honestly stunned at being here. It seemed illogical to me. Illogical, arbitrary and at moments plainly pointless. At a time in which the moral absolute of genocide raged, what was the experience of a young Jew, shielded from the outside world, when he clashed with reality?

Luckily you cannot go back in time, return to the brightest moments of those childhood years. Never. That wish, that idea is a real Tantalus' torment to many. Understandable, when you see how hopelessly wrong and ambiguous the average Westerner presents the representation of life and death to his descendants. Almost everyone behaves as if we all enjoy eternal life! We are all young, beautiful and well-to-do. Nobody gets sick and if that does unexpectedly happen, medication promptly offers a solution. Instinctively, a child feels that this representation is not true to the facts, yet only when the unavoidable confrontation hits you cold in the face, it is there: death. Sudden, rough, hard. A breaking point. It would be immensely more sensible to make everybody understand how sudden life can end. Not only would people be stimulated to think more about their actions, it would also help each and every one to develop a personal view on death and dying. Useful and wise. How else can you grow old serenely? By *not* thinking about your mortality? That looks too much like the starting point for a guaranteed tragic existence.

Alas, the Westerner has not only forgotten how to mourn and unlearned a sense of the tragedy of life. Our culture does not manage to deal in a dignified way with the pure essence of our existence either. An essence, many feel, that should best remain concealed, because man is what he conceals and what he conceals is his mortality. Western man would do well to carry the awareness of his ephemerality with dignity, each new day. Death is not sad. Not absolute. All the same it is healing and puts things into perspective, which is a help in realizing that all problems and happiness end one day. The feeling of being uprooted, part of the notion of 'home', would also disappear. Because what is dying other than the final homecoming?

But before that time has come, the artist most naturally wants to finalize his story: that one book, that one song. Obsessive, almost neurotic, you continue. Till the last rose of your summer flowers. While working you transform dreams into reality. Intense, and with Beckett's motto in mind: *'Fail, fail again, fail better.'* For a nomad of language, it is unthinkable to ever distance oneself from the axiom, let alone preach cynicism. Your work stands in reality, does not allow even for one second that the near goodbye would mist your eyes but a second. Stubbornly, you choose to go on reporting, regardless of whether you are forty or seventy. Of course, you have a sound notion of mortality. The cultural historian in any serious author wakes up at regular intervals, exploring the frontiers of science – exact or not – and of non-fiction that threatens to turn into fiction as it is written down.

As an artist, you live in the conviction that fifty years from now, a hundred years at the most, you will be totally, utterly and completely forgotten. A cultural archaeologist might just happen to incidentally turn up your name while weeding through some old documents, DVDs, or whatever new-fangled archival system they will have then. A sobering thought? Yes. Discouraging? No. A well-developed feel for temporality can even increase your feeling of freedom in no small measure. The core of world literature consists mainly of dark sighs and endless whining about the finiteness of our existence. Challenging fatality in that light testifies to superior detachment. In the very dark *Closing Time*, Cohen sang about *'the awful truth, which you can't reveal to the ears of youth'*. Nearly ten years later, he estimated that his listeners were ripe enough to make them part of a few horrible truths. And so he admits that in many numbers of *Ten New Songs* death is prominently present. Leonard Cohen, without a trace of self-complaint:

*'That is the ocean you swim in as you get older. I think any man of 67 has a pretty clear idea that, you know, the sense of limitation is acute.'*

### 'Undress your heart'

When the time of earthly pleasures small and big is walking on its last legs and a bitter bedtime story seems to be in order, the last masks fall. For many it is the moment of the final confrontation with the eye of God. He, that bookkeeper of death, does not pay attention to religious contrivance. When death comes, the person balancing at the precipice of life in mortal fear cannot make abstraction of the situation and judge with a clear head. He or she only wants to clear the heart from all ballast, free it for its very last journey.

*Ah the wind, the wind is blowing*
*Through the graves the wind is blowing*
*Freedom soon will come*
*Then we'll come from the shadow*
Marly in H. Zaret

April in December. It must be the ideal last wish. Let it storm. Let it freeze. Let it rain. To renege on your finality is not an option. We are the woods in which a lot has been felled. Life has been lived. There is no need for tears. Letting go of all your ambitions is a relief. Your willingness to be killed in action a fact. Then the sun comes shining through from behind the clouds. Like the character in *The Scream* of Munch you lash out one last time. A scream in which you compact language and poetry, words and music. It is the definitive goodbye, your obituary card. A new journey awaits. *Oh Mort, vieux capitaine, il est temps! Levons l'ancre!* (Oh Death, old captain, it is time! Lift the anchor!)

*that twenty centuries*
*breathlessly elapsed*
*and in his heart*
*antique peace*
*had settled*
Hendrik Marsman

He who wants to fathom life must understand three things, according to the Indian philosopher Krishnamurti: time, sorrow, and death. Life cannot be without its death. Apollonian or narrow-minded, timeless or measured... death is our atonal final chord. Leonard Cohen, beautiful loser *par excellence*, has accepted this. There is no need for hyperboles or staged reality. The earthly truth please, and with it ultimate redemption. If – detached and sober – you have an eye for it, you might even be able to enjoy it.

*Like a bird on the wire*
*Like a drunk in a midnight choir*
*I have tried in my way*
*to be free*
Leonard Cohen

*I wrote the book I had to write...*
*Having read it,*
*I hope it will enable you to listen to*
*the old songs with new ears*
Marc Hendrickx

AFTERMATH

Having finished the 'first version' of my book's text shortly after the turn of the century, I gladly put it aside to focus on the other elements which I had planned alongside the writing itself, before returning to the latter. I desperately wanted to give the release of *Yesterday's Tomorrow* a full project approach.

First up were the recordings for a brand-new CD by a popular (Belgian) artist, containing modern versions of several of the main songs receiving attention in *Yesterday's Tomorrow*. Giving my book an accompanying 'soundtrack', so to speak. This book-CD combination would then become the basis of a theatre tour, hitting venues when the twosome would be launched. All went perfectly well.

An additional idea was to take the concept one step further still and capture the whole process of how book, CD and tour came about in a filmed documentary. Not only did I find a company sufficiently interested to start this project, Mr. Cohen himself was kind enough to grant me permission to go film inside his Hydra home in the company of his daughter, Lorca.

In the end, all *Yesterday's Tomorrow* enterprises undertaken would come to fruition, bar one – the TV documentary, which did not garner enough interest from television networks. Regardless, the work done on Hydra, both inside Leonard Cohen's retreat and while addressing a group of Cohenites – Cohen fans – with the artists delivering songs from the soundtrack CD's imbued the first Belgian and Dutch editions of *Yesterday's Tomorrow* with additional depth and feeling.

Not too long after the great-but-tiring launch and performances surrounding the *Yesterday's Tomorrow* releases in Belgium and The Netherlands, news broke out that Mr. Cohen's manager of many years, Ms. Kelley Lynch, had robbed her boss of virtually all of his retirement savings. In true gentleman's fashion, greatly helped by years of Zen Buddhist training, the artist commented on what happened with dry wit, saying *"Maybe it's a good thing... It will get the old man working again"*. And it did.

Years ago this situation would have led to anxiety and fear in Cohen. Not this time. It did, however, spark a creative flame within him. *Book of Longing*, a new collection of poems, had already been scheduled for release, but – being a poetry collection – could hardly be expected to aid financially. Then again, the artist still had his houses and other possessions, ongoing income from record sales, as well as royalties derived from new cover versions recorded by a myriad list of artists. Taking all of that into account, combined with his utterly modest needs and lifestyle, which did not depart all that much from his Zen days *'up on the hill'* of Mount Baldy, the ill-informed criticism which some levelled at Cohen's comeback, as if it were nothing but a money-driven enterprise out of desperate need, was laughable.

Far closer to reality was that his new financial status spurred Leonard Cohen on, yes, as he did want to further remedy the situation. But no one, the old master included, could ever have predicted what the grand finale would lead to. That was totally unforeseen, impossible to predict and nearly miraculous!

Not one to arrive at the start of a battle unprepared, nor one to take chances, Leonard Cohen and a carefully selected crew of old (Neil Larsen, Sharon Robinson, Roscoe Beck, Bob Metzger) and new (Charley and Hattie Webb, the Webb sisters, Rafael Gayol, Dino Soldo, Javier Maz) musical friends painstakingly prepared for the artist's first concerts in well over fifteen years. Making sure the wait would be worth it, Cohen & C° went for an extensive stage-scape. The amount of equipment impressive (most band members being multi-instrumentalists), they opted to tour with their own sound system and light show to boot. Not having to use house equipment, this ruled out any possible technical hiccups. Hiring top notch sound and light engineers, able to deliver crystal-clear sound and video in virtually every big or small hall or in open air put the icing on the cake. They practiced every night until they were ready!

The première of Leonard Cohen performing live in the 21st century was not announced with a lot of fanfare. Neither did it take place in a renowned hall in one of the world's leading entertainment capitals. Rather, modest Fredericton, a remote Canadian city with a population of a mere 50,000 inhabitants, got the honor. There, on an evening in May 2008, Leonard Cohen, dressed in his trademark Armani suit and Fedora hat, walked out on stage for the first time in what must have felt like ages. The audience in the packed auditorium immediately rose to its feet and started a two-minute ovation. The artist responded by softly reciting a poem verse in French, after which the band broke into *Dance Me to the End of Love*.

Throughout the next few hours, the beautiful musical sparseness that Cohen's lyrics request, as well as the accompaniment by female voices which makes them hit home when blended in with his own delivery in rich and deep tones were omnipresent. Accolades were earned by all concerned, not least for musical director Roscoe Beck and the sound man, who transferred the experience on stage to the audience, making it sound as if they were all listening to a recording played over a massive stereo sound system. Each member of the band was given more than one chance to shine by the main man, which lead to memorable moments, etching themselves deep into people's memories. Few visitors will have gone home without a vivid image of Javier Maz's impressive intro to *Who By Fire*, Dino Soldo's uncharacteristically headbanging, while losing himself in the music, or the Webb sisters' extraordinary vocals during a reverent *If It Be Your Will*. Overall, the audience was mesmerized. They laughed, whistled and screamed multiple times, enjoyed the fun moments when Leonard Cohen underscored their connection through a humorous statement, and they occasionally wiped a tear from the corner of their eyes, taken as they were by the sheer intensity and emotion of the experience.

No longer was there any doubt whether being on tour again was a good idea. Out of the window too, the fear that maybe the following that had been there during the last full-blown tour some twenty years earlier could possibly have evaporated. Following ten sold out performances on Canadian soil, the unified hearts touring band was well and truly ready to start conquering the world. The first step abroad being Dublin, Ireland, within days to be followed by two most illustrious festivals: reputed Montreux Jazz Festival and massive Glastonbury.

What nobody had expected happened almost overnight. Leonard Cohen live, about as much the opposite of a dynamic modern day pop/rock show as possible, not featuring any stage props, special effects, costume changes or whatever trickery, became the number one event that people flocked to. All through that summer and fall, the European continent played host to a massive number of Cohen shows. In early 2009 New Zealand, Australia and North America followed suit. After which the ongoing request to please return led to yet more European and North American dates. A particularly triumphant occasion being the staging of a special show *"for reconciliation, tolerance and peace"* in Tel Aviv, Israel, at which well over 50,000 people turned up.

For many a faithful Leonard Cohen follower, the immense adoration which now befell their old hero was quite hard to fathom. Where did all those people come from? How come thousands and thousands flocked to see a 75-year-old poet and singer-songwriter that the masses had paid no attention to for decades? Any explanation that made sense proved very hard to come by. After all, Cohen now played shows in massive concert halls for throngs of people, but in no way did he achieve this extraordinary new status by selling out artistically.

The latter was soon to be underpinned, Cohen's renaissance not to remain entirely based upon his work of old.

First off, *Poems and Songs* offered a new collection in writing. Then *Old Ideas* appeared, a brand-new set of ten songs. Racing up the pop music charts in a widespread collection of over thirty-five countries, it set plenty of records (Cohen as the oldest artist ever to hit #1 on a large number of charts, his album marking the longest gap in-between two #1's, etc.). What surprised even more was the actual merit of the album. Its contribution to Leonard Cohen's legacy.

Ever the self-mocking *'little Jew'*, Cohen opened it in his most low-down voice. Poking fun at his status as the suave gentleman, forever using eloquent wording, he wryly described himself as *'a sportsman and a shepherd, a lazy bastard living in a suit.'* And that was just the beginning. His lyrics showed off effortlessly that the old master had not lost his touch nor the ability to offer yet another fine take on some favorite subjects. *Anyhow* showcasing the bleakness of love gone bad, *The Darkness* being exactly that, whereas *Come Healing* indeed offered the penitential hymn which it promised.

What made *Old Ideas* even more relevant, was that Cohen went out on tour again and gave an elaborate selection of the album's songs central placing in his shows. Each of them easily held their own, next to true *monstre sacrés*, songs that had been pillars of his catalogue for decades. As such, the new string of shows were a telling testimony to the fact that, to an artist, age is nothing but a number, just as long as the fire within is still burning. The new string of concerts started off with five open air concerts. Unforgettable evenings in Ghent, Belgium, where well over 80,000 people turned up and filled St. Peter's Square to the very last seat, while several of those who had failed to get tickets went as far as to climb up in the trees.

Having played countries throughout Europe, states in the U.S. and cities in Canada, Cohen returned to the old continent once more in the summer of 2013. He rounded off that leg of the tour in Amsterdam on the night before his 80th birthday, being forced to allow for a little break in the midst of his performance when the 17,000 present broke into a hearty

*Happy Birthday*. Following a few weeks off, he and his band concluded their second worldwide tour in five years with a final sixteen concerts in Australia and New-Zealand.

Long-term fans having been spoiled rotten by a virtual overdose (next to the concerts, the new poetry work and the new CD, multiple live releases came out too), and the general public more acutely aware of Leonard Cohen than ever, 2014 appeared pretty quiet at first. *Popular Problems*, a new CD released in September that year, could not really chase away that feeling, despite selling just as madly as *Old Ideas*. The album simply did not register the same impact as its predecessor. Partly because the astonishment of seeing a man approaching eighty release a more than worthwhile collection of songs the second time around is just not as impressive as experiencing such a feat for the first time. Also, there were no live presentations to help the songs establish a place in people's minds and hearts. Lastly though, one can only ascertain that the material, well-written, varied and well-performed by all involved as it was, simply was not as strong as what was featured on the former album. *Nevermind* being a notable exception. Not even the surprisingly uncharacteristically optimistic *You Got Me Singing* could conceal that fact.

Quite ironically in the light of all that went on in years before, Leonard Cohen was now regarded as a stronghold by his record company. And so, there was to be no letup in the string of releases. New, expanded editions of his classic albums came out, as well as *Can't Forget – A Souvenir of the Grand Tour*. The latter including some noteworthy new songs, written on tour and rehearsed during soundchecks, alongside live recordings of some of his own classics and a cover of *La Manic*, Georges Dor's fine ode to his loved one, living nearby Québec's Lake Manicouagan.

Meanwhile, Cohen's health suffered a major setback. Whereas the leukemia which plagued the artist had never prohibited him from functioning as he wished, a severe back injury now did, as did – to quote how the artist himself thought about it – *"other disagreeable visitations"*. The situation having become intolerable, Cohen abandoned all work on his next album. Resuming it only after interference by his son, Adam, who arranged for a medical chair which allowed the elder Cohen to sit and sing. Working with the material recorded by his father and long-term musical collaborator Patrick Leonard, who by an uncanny coincidence was also out due to a back problem, Adam Cohen took over production work of the new album. Adding both a classical touch (in the form of a choral arrangement and an impressive contribution by Cantor Gideon Y. Zelermyer and the Congregation Shaar Hashomayim Synagogue Choir) and a modern one (by having the album wrapped in a cover and accompanied by an album booklet by Belgian art designer Sammy Slabbinck) Adam Cohen helped his father to lift *You Want it Darker* up to a very high standard.

The title track's bleak setting, the content of songs such as *Leaving the Table* and *Travelling Light* seemingly hinting at a goodbye or farewell of sorts, led a number of people to perceive the newest Cohen release as a possible last album. A vision that was enforced even further when news broke of Marianne Ihlen's passing, and the fact that Leonard Cohen had written a farewell note to support her in her last days, in which he had stated that he would not be too long behind.

Confronted with this during the record's release press conference, he denied in characteristically self-deprecating modus: *"I said I was ready to die, recently. I think I was exaggerating (chuckles). One is given to self-dramatization from time to time. I intend to live forever."* His untimely death less than three weeks later may, at first glance, appeared to have contradicted his words. It certainly reinforced the feeling of many that Cohen meant *You Want it Darker* to intentionally contain his final words, just as David Bowie's *Black Star* had one year earlier.

As always in such matters, there is not just one single, all-encompassing truth. Of course, the artist was more than aware of the shortcomings of his ageing body in the final year of his life. Cohen had already expressed at 67 years old how much he realized that his time on earth was running out. Given the nature of his writing, this caused more end of life sentiments to find their way into his lyrics fifteen years on. That said, it was equally obvious to all close to him, that ever since his depressions lifted and he accepted his position as a songwriter, Leonard Cohen thoroughly enjoyed life. It brought him great joy in the new century, both artistically and in private, where it was a privilege for all of those present to see how he reveled in his double role as a doting father and mischievous granddad.

Leonard Cohen will indeed live forever. Looking back on all that happened since the initial release of *Yesterday's Tomorrow* back in 2004, it is really kind of bizarre that in those days, this book was born out of sheer necessity. As a means to try and prove that the writing which this unique man invested the best part of nearly half a decade in, had value and would last in the future. Starting a mere four years later, millions of people would go to see Leonard Cohen perform live. More still bought his new albums, DVDs, best of compilations or rehashed versions of his older releases. And will continue to do so as new work will continue to be released in the future.

Yet, *Yesterday's Tomorrow* is here again too. Why? First and foremost because with all that happened, there is a new legion of people listening to and reading Leonard Cohen. Secondly, there is a group of people who simply missed the book the first time around. But also, lastly and most endearing to me as its writer, because *Yesterday's Tomorrow* contributed in its own very small and modest way to help preserve the fundamental worth of Mr. Cohen's work at a time when the need for such a preservation act was palpable. And because today, *Yesterday's Tomorrow* has become a tiny piece of what has by now turned into a very large puzzle itself. A piece which I hope you, as its reader, will have enjoyed discovering.

NOT ME, BUT THE OTHERS…

Quite obviously *Yesterday's Tomorrow* is infused with the influence that Cohen's work has had on me as a writer, year after year. Apart from this, other, less Cohen-inspired influences and people played their part. I should thank them effusively, and where possible I gladly do this, even though it is not always clear who or what lay at the basis of certain thoughts and ideas. Allow me to rejoice in this… not everything needs an explanation!

Those people I can mention by name and first name, you will find on the next page. Accept from me in good faith that the attention which I attribute to them is far too limited.

Next to those sources of inspiration, people close to me in everyday life also played an important part. However practical some contacts may be, at first glance largely distanced from my writing, I simply could not continue to keep blackening the pages if their presence, help and moral support was not there all along. As most prefer to keep out of the limelight even more than I do, I'll refrain from mentioning their names. That said, my gratitude to those wonderful examples of the so-hard-to-understand species we call *homo sapien,* wonderful in mind, in body, in both, is sheer endless.

*Marc Hendrickx*

## INSPIRATION, TRANSPIRATION, SAMPLES AND HALLUCINATION

Just to say that a book like this drinks from many a source. Things that have to be said impose themselves, invite you to pursue them, are consciously or subconsciously picked up and blow in without telling you where they originated from. Undoing the puzzle and looking for who, what and where is a sheer hopeless and unnecessary task. Artistic honesty does imply though that wherever possible specifically consulted sources be mentioned. So here goes:

### _Realisations of Leonard Cohen since the initial/first edition of 'Yesterday's Tomorrow'_

2018 – The Flame – Poems and Selections from Notebooks (McClelland and Stewart Ltd, Canada)

2016 – You Want it Darker (CD, CBS, USA)

2015 – Can't Forget – A Souvenir from the Grand Tour (CD, CBS, USA)

2014 – Popular Problems (CD, CBS, USA)

2014 – Live in Dublin (Blu-Ray, DVD, 3CD CBS, USA)

2012 – Fifteen Poems (E-book)

2012 – Live in Fredericton (EP, CD, CBS, USA)

2012 – Old Ideas (CD, CBS, USA)

2011 – Poems and Songs (McClelland and Stewart Ltd, Canada)

2010 – Songs from the Road (DVD, CD, CBS, USA)

2009 – Live at the Isle of Wight (DVD, 2LP, CBS, USA)

2009 – Live in London (DVD, 2CD, CBS, USA)

2006 – Book of Longing (McClelland and Stewart Ltd, Canada)

### **Already existing when** _'Yesterday's Tomorrow' was written_

2004 – _Dear Heather_ (CD, CBS, USA)

2002 – *The Essential Leonard Cohen* (2 CDs, CBS, USA)

2001 – *Ten New Songs* (CD, CBS, USA)

2001 – *Field Commander Cohen – Tour of 1979* (CD, CBS, USA)

1997 – *More Best of Leonard Cohen* (CD, CBS, USA)

1994 – *Cohen Live!* (CD, CBS, USA)

1993 – *Stranger Music* (Poetry and song lyrics, McClelland and Stewart Ltd, Canada)

1992 – *The Future* (CD, CBS, USA)

1988 – *I'm Your Man* (LP, CBS, USA)

1984 – *Various Positions* (LP, CBS, England)

1984 – *Book of Mercy* (Psalms, McClelland and Stewart Ltd, Canada)

1979 – *Recent Songs* (LP, CBS, USA)

1978 – *Death of a Lady's Man* (Poetry, McClelland and Stewart Ltd, Canada)

1977 – *Death of a Ladies' Man* (LP, CBS, USA)

1975 – *Greatest Hits* (LP, CBS, USA)

1974 – *New Skin for the Old Ceremony* (LP, CBS, USA)

1973 – *Live Songs* (LP, CBS, USA)

1972 – *The Energy of Slaves* (Poetry, McClelland and Stewart Ltd, Canada)

1971 – *Songs of Love and Hate* (LP, CBS, USA)

1969 – *Songs From a Room* (LP, CBS, USA)

1968 – *Selected Poems: 1956 –1968* (Poetry, McClelland and Stewart Ltd., Canada)

1967 – *Songs of Leonard Cohen* (LP, CBS, USA)

1966 – *Parasites of Heaven* (Poetry, McClelland and Stewart Ltd, Canada)

1966 – *Beautiful Losers* (Novel, McClelland and Stewart Ltd, Canada)

1964 – *Flowers for Hitler* (Poetry, McClelland and Stewart Ltd, Canada)

1963 – *The Favourite Game* (Novel, Secker and Warburg Ltd, England)

1961 – *The Spice-Box of Earth* (Poetry, McClelland and Stewart Ltd, Canada)

1956 – *Let Us Compare Mythologies* (Poetry, Contact Press, Canada)

Apart from this list, Leonard Cohen also contributed to the work of other artists. The most famous example of these is Jennifer Warnes' *Famous Blue Raincoat* (CD from 1986), yet the old master also had a cameo performance in an episode of *Miami Vice* and did a guest vocal on *Elvis's Rolls Royce* (a track on the *Are you Okay?* CD of Was Not Was); not to be forgotten either is the musical *Night Magic*, a project for which Mr. Cohen penned all texts (1984). Another remarkable item was his recitation, two videos long, of texts for an edition of *The Tibetan Book of The Dead* in 1996.

An exhaustive bibliography/discography can be found on the site http://www.Leonardcohenfiles.com.

There you will also find an impressive survey of books about Leonard Cohen, his work and his life, next to an even more impressive amount of tangential information.

### Consulted TV documentaries and films about or by Leonard Cohen

1997 – *Leonard Cohen – Spring 1996* (A. Brusq, France)

1996 – *In Short* (A compilation of four short films, Canada)

1988 – *Songs from the Life of Leonard Cohen* (BBC, England)

1984 – *I Am a Hotel* (A. Nicholls, Canada)

1981 – *The Song of Leonard Cohen* (H. Rasky, Canada)

1974 – *Bird on a Wire* (L. Cohen, USA)

1965 – *Ladies and Gentlemen – Mr. Leonard Cohen* (CBC, Canada)

### Consulted books about, or directly connected to Leonard Cohen

2001 – *The Song of Leonard Cohen* (H. Rasky, Mosaic Press, Canada)

1996 – *Various Positions – A Life of Leonard Cohen* (I. Nadel, Random House, Canada)

1996 – *In Every Style of Passion* ( J. Devlin, Omnibus Press, England)

1996 – *Partisan der Liebe* (C. Graf, VGS Verlagsgesell-schaft, Germany)

1994 – *Leonard Cohen – A Life in Art* (I. Nadel, ECW Press, Germany)

1990 – *Prophet of the Heart* (L.S. Dorman and C.L. Rawlins, Omnibus Press, England)\*

1974 – *Leonard Cohen* ( J. Vassal et J.D. Brierre, Albin Michel, France)

## Consulted non-Cohen-related sources of inspiration

2002 – *Verzamelde gedichten* (H. Marsman, Athenaeum–Polak & Van Gennep, The Netherlands)

2002 – *Verzamelde gedichten* ( J.C. Bloem, Athenaeum–Polak & Van Gennep, The Netherlands)

2000 – *Berichten uit Kolyma* (V. Sjalamov, Busy Bee, The Netherlands)

1964 – *Sleeping With One Eye Open* (M. Strand, Atheneum, USA)

## As if it had been made especially for me

1971 – *Warnung vor einer heiligen Nutte* (Rainer Werner Fassbinder, Germany)

---

\*        This is the only Cohen-related book from which a quotation has been taken. It is duly mentioned in the relevant chapter (Chapter 1 – The Guests)

## Passers-by

*(People who in one way or another influenced the text, in order of appearance)*

Durante Alighieri Dante, Henry David Thoreau, Giorgio van Straten, Marguerite Yourcenar, A. F.Th. Van der Heijden, Jeanette Winterson, Hendrik Marsman, Karl Marx, György Konrad, Arthur Schopenhauer, Friedrich Nietzsche, Willem Frederik Hermans, F. Scott Fitzgerald, Michel Onfray, Ramses Shaffy, Bruce Springsteen, James Dean, Marcel Proust, Aristotle, René Magritte, Plato, Paul Valéry, Hermann Hesse, Georg Hegel, Johann Wolfgang von Goethe, Ludwig Wittgenstein, Louis-Ferdinand Céline, Oscar Wilde, H. Westbroek, Sören Kierkegaard, Paul De Wispelaere, Remco Campert, Emily Dickinson, Yann Martel, Cesare Pavese, Arnon Grunberg, Tom Waits, Nicholas Berdyaev, George Ivan Van Morrison, Edmund Burke, Jacques Brel, Max Frisch, André Breton, Joris-Karl Huysmans, Piet Gerbrandy, Tennessee Williams, Richard Klink- hamer, Ernest Hemingway, Samuel Beckett, Edvard Munch, Charles Baudelaire, Jiddu Krishnamurti.

*Taken from different works, used with permission*

In # 2: The poem 'Keeping Things Whole' by Mark Strand, quoted with permission of the author, from *Sleeping With One Eye Open* (Atheneum, 1964)

In When the devil… A fragment from the poem 'November' by Jacobus Cornelis Bloem, quoted with permission by the editor, from *Verzamelde gedichten* (Athenaeum, Polak & Van Gennep, 2002)

In # 7: A fragment from the poem 'De onvoltooide tempel' by Hendrik Marsman, quoted with permission of the publisher from *Verzamelde*

*Quotes from interviews with Leonard Cohen, used under the free right of quotation*

In # 1: *The Boston Globe*, journalist Jeff McLaughlin.

In # 2: *Interview Magazine*, as interviewed by Anjelica Huston

In # 2: *Entertainment Weekly*, journalist David Browne.

In # 2: *Leonard Cohen, Spring 1996*, journalist Amélie Brusq

In # 2: *Guardian Unlimited Observer/Life*, journalist Nick Paton Walsh

In # 2: *Musician*, journalist Mark Rowland

In # 2: *NME*, journalist Alastair Pirrie

In # 2: *Songtalk*, journalist Paul Zollo

In # 2: CBC, journalist Moses Znaimer

In # 3: *Los Angeles Times Sunday*, journalist Robert Hilburn

In # 3: France 2 TV 'Le cercle de minuit', journalist Michel Field

In # 3: *Toronto Globe and Mail*, journalist Doug Sanders

In # 3: *London Daily Mail*, journalist Spencer Bright

In # 3: *One on One*, journalist Barbara Gowdy

In # 3: *Les Inrockuptibles*, journalist Christian Fevret

In # 3: *ABC Sunday Supplement*, journalist Jordi Saladrigas

In # 3: *Euroman*, journalist Martin Oestergaard

In Genesis: *Les Inrockuptibles*, journalist Christian Fevret

In # 4: Internet Chat Transcript, 2001

In # 4: CBC, journalist Moses Znaimer

In # 4: *Yakety Yak*, journalist Scott Cohen

In # 4: *Les Inrockuptibles*, journalist Gilles Tordjman

In # 4 : *Leonard Cohen*, journalist Robert Sward

In # 4: *La Vanguardia*, journalist Javier Laborda

In # 4: *The Jewish Book News Interview*, journalists Arthur Kurzweil and Pamela Roth

In # 4: *Leonard Cohen*, journalist Diethard Küster

In # 4: *Buzz*, journalist Pico Iver

In # 4: *Interview Magazine*, as interviewed by Anjelica Huston

In # 4: *The Daily Telegraph*, journalist Tim Rostron

In # 4: *Guardian Unlimited Observer / Life*, journalist Nick Paton Walsh

In # 4: *Los Angeles Times Sunday*, journalist Robert Hilburn

In # 5: *Songtalk*, journalist Paul Zollo

In # 5: *Leonard Cohen – Spring 1996*, journalist Amélie Brusq

In # 5: *Rolling Stone*, journalist Anthony DeCurtis

In # 5: *Sounds*, journalist Billy Walker

In # 5: *NME*, journalist Gavin Martin

In # 5: *Toronto Globe and Mail*, journalist Doug Sanders

In # 5: *Maclean's*, journalist Brian D. Johnson

In # 5: *Goldmine*, journalist William Ruhlmann

In # 5: *Melody Maker*, journalist Elizabeth Thomson

In # 6: *Expresso*, journalist João Lisboa

In # 6: *Maclean's*, journalist Brian D. Johnson

In # 6: *Blitz*, journalist John Wilde

In # 6: *Ziggurat*, journalist Serge Simonart

In # 6: *Leonard Cohen, Spring 1996*, journalist Amélie Brusq

In # 6: *Songtalk*, journalist Paul Zollo

In # 6: *Buzz*, interview Pico Iver

In When the devil...: *Leonard Cohen, Spring 1996*, journalist Amélie Brusq

In When the devil...: *Leonard Cohen*, journalist Diethard Küster

In When the devil...: *Sincerely L. Cohen*, journalist Brian Cullman

In When the devil...: *Euroman*, journalist Martin

Oestergaard

 In When the devil…: *The Observer*, journalist Alan Jackson
 In When the devil…: *NME*, journalist Gavin Martin In When the devil…: *Saturday Night Online*, journalist Mireille Silcott

 In # 7: *The New York Observer*, journalist Frank DiGiacomo

## COMING OF AGE WITH LEONARD COHEN

It has been a while, say quite a while, since I felt this for the first time: having to write, with all-time favorite Leonard Cohen as a source of inspiration. Not the kind of writer to run away with himself, adept at the 'less is more' philosophy and recognized amateur of godly wines that need years to mature, the Jewish-Canadian grandmaster would certainly agree that time can never be a measuring stick. But, all right, it has been done. I have made the transition from working with icons and social movements to an extremely individual, almost anonymous experience. I feel good about it. What I can hope for now is that you – the reader, unknown to me – can share the experience with me and emerge touched from it, in one way or another.

*Marc Hendrickx*

<u>*Trajectory of the author*</u>

<u>*Realizations since the initial 'Yesterday's Tomorrow'*</u>

2019 – Muhammad Ali – Nog altijd de Grootste! (Xander, Netherlands, special edition by popular demand)

2018 – *Libertijns België* (Willems Uitgevers, Belgium)

2018 – Theatre play *'De erfenis van de Koning'*, with Michael Vroemans

2018 – Theatre play *'Op weg naar WEMBELIE!'* with Dirk Dobbeleers

2017 – *Elvis dichtbij* (Willems Uitgevers, Belgium)

2016 – *Muhammad Ali – Nog altijd de Grootste!* (Xander, Netherlands, fully revised edition)

2016 – *Elvis Presley, Richard Nixon and the American Dream* (McFarland & Company, USA, with Connie Kirchberg, re-edition)

2015 – Man in de Marge (De Vries – Brouwers, Belgium)

2014 – Full length movie and accompanying book *Booster* (Abimo, Belgium, with Dirk Dobbeleers - adaptation of the youth novel *'Wolken en een beetje regen', see 2005)*

2013 – *Heb jij ze wel alle vijf?* (Abimo, Belgium, with Dirk Dobbeleers, youth novel)

2012 – Theatre play *'Den Derby 2'*, with Dirk Dobbeleers

2011 – *Nuages* (Abimo, Belgium, with Dirk Dobbeleers, youth novel – French language version of *'Wolken en een beetje regen', see 2005*)

2011 – *Angie – Anders dan de anderen* (Kramat, Belgium, young adult novel)

2010 – *Muhammad Ali – Nog altijd de Grootste!* (Linkeroever, Belgium, re-edition)

2010 – *Wapenland* (Abimo, Belgium, with Dirk Dobbeleers, youth novel)

2009 – Theatre play *'Den Derby'*, with Dirk Dobbeleers

2009 – Theatre play *'CoopmanCampioen!'*, with Dirk Dobbeleers

2008 – *Getreinde wanhoop* (Abimo, Belgium, with Dirk Dobbeleers, new edition)

2008 – *Yesterday's Tomorrow* (Guerra & Paz, Portugal)

2008 – *Yesterday's Tomorrow* (Milenio, Spain)

2008 – *Yesterday's Tomorrow* (Brandl & Schlesinger, Australia)

2007 – *Elvis A. Presley – Muziek, Mens, Mythe* (Vanhalewyck, Belgium, fully revised edition)

2007 – *Ma, pa, puinhoop!?* (Abimo, Belgium, with Dirk Dobbeleers, youth novel) + French language version (Mols, Belgium)

### Already existing when the initial *'Yesterday's Tomorrow'* was written

2005 – *Wolken en een beetje regen* (Abimo, Belgium, with Dirk Dobbeleers, youth novel)

2004 – *Yesterday's Tomorrow* (Vanhalewyck, Belgium)

2003 – *Getreinde wanhoop* (Houtekiet, Belgium, with Dirk Dobbeleers, first youth novel)

2003 – *Elvis A. Presley – Die Musik, der Mensch, der Mythos* (Hannibal, Germany, completely revised reprint)

2002 – *Muhammad Ali – Nog altijd de Grootste!* (Houtekiet, Belgium)

2000 – *Fawltymania!* (QM, The Netherlands, completely revised reprint, with Rudy Van Heuven)

1999 – *Elvis Presley, Richard Nixon and the American Dream* (McFarland & Company, USA, with Connie Kirchberg)

1998 – *Elvis A. Presley – Musique et vie d'un mythe* (Atlas, France, adaptation into a series)

1998 – *Elvis A. Presley – Muziek, Mens, Mythe* (QM, The Netherlands, revised reprint)

1997 – *Gaia – Profiel van een beweging* (Icarus/De Standaard, Belgium)

1996 – *Fawltymania!* (MBP, Belgium, with Rudy Van Heuven)

1996 – *Keith – Het genie naast Mick Jagger* (MBP, Belgium, adaptation from an English language bio)

1994 – Debut as a writer at Coda Publishers, Belgium, in both Belgian languages (Flemish/French): *Elvis A. Presley – Muziek, Mens, Mythe &*

*Elvis A. Presley – Musique et vie d'un mythe*

1981 – First official publication which the author contributed to. The beginning of a period of ten years of 'preparation', before he would actually become an author. A period in which he assisted in the making of countless books and magazine contributions with and for other authors.